Bluegrass Fakebook
by
Bert Casey

On the cover: Renfroe Valley Barn Dance Band, circa 1947.
Left to right: Croy Gibbs, Slim Miller, Clay Eager, Granny Harper, Claude Sweet, Tommy Covington

Table of Contents

Ain't Gonna Work Tomorrow	1	Glendale Train	41
All The Good Times Are Past & Gone	2	God Moves In A Windstorm *	42
Amazing Grace *	3	Going Down That Road Feeling Bad	43
Angel Band *	4	Gone At Last	44
Angels Rejoice *	5	Good Woman's Love	45
Are You Washed In The Blood *	6	Goodnight Irene	46
Banks of the Ohio	7	Green Pastures *	47
Battle of New Orleans	8	Hallelujah I'm Ready *	48
Beautiful Life *	9	He Said If I Be Lifted Up *	49
Bluebirds Are Singing For Me	10	He Will Set Your Fields On Fire *	50
Boil Them Cabbage Down	11	He's Got The Whole World In His Hands *	51
Born To Be With You	12	High On A Mountain	52
Bound To Ride	13	Hobo Song	53
Bury Me Beneath The Willows	14	Hot Corn, Cold Corn	54
Careless Love	15	I Ain't Broke (But I'm Badly Bent)	55
Children Go Where I Send Thee *	16	I Am A Pilgrim *	56
Columbus Stockade Blues	17	I Never Will Marry	57
Cripple Creek	18	I'll Fly Away *	58
Crying Holy *	19	I'll Remember You, Love, In My Prayers *	59
Dancin With The Angels *	20	If I Lose	60
Daniel Prayed *	21	In The Pines	61
Dark Hollow	22	It Won't Work This Time	62
Darling Corey	23	Jacob's Vision *	63
Do Lord *	24	Jesse James	64
Don't This Road Look Rough & Rocky	25	John Hardy	65
Don't You Hear Jerusalem Moan *	26	John Henry	66
Dooley	27	Jordan *	67
Down The Road	28	Katy Daley	68
Drifting Too Far From The Shore *	29	Kneel Down & Pray Up *	69
Dry Run Creek	30	Knockin' On Your Door	70
East Virginia Blues	31	Last Train From Poor Valley	71
Every Time You Say Goodbye	32	Legend of the Rebel Soldier	72
Fair & Tender Ladies	33	Life Is Like A Mountain Railway *	73
Find Me Out On A Mountain Top	34	Like A Train	74
Foggy Mountain Top	35	Little Bessie	75
Footprints In The Snow	36	Little Maggie	76
Freeborn Man	37	Little White Church *	77
Friend of the Devil	38	Long Journey Home	78
Get In Line Brother *	39	Lord, I'm Coming Home *	79
Ginseng Sullivan	40	Lost & I'll Never Find The Way	80

Mama Don't 'Low	81	Swing Low, Sweet Chariot *	123
Man of Constant Sorrow	82	Take Me In Your Lifeboat *	124
Memories of Mother and Dad *	83	Talk About Suffering *	125
Methodist Pie *	84	Tennessee Stud	126
Midnight Flyer	85	There's More Pretty Girls Than One	127
Midnight on the Stormy Deep	86	Think of What You've Done	128
Midnight Train	87	This World Is Not My Home *	129
Milwaukee Here I Come	88	Tom Dooley	130
Model Church *	89	Train, Train	131
Moonlight Midnight	90	Troubles Up & Down The Road	132
My Home's Across The Smoky Mountains	91	Turn Your Radio On *	133
New River Train	92	Uncloudy Day *	134
Nine Pound Hammer	93	Wabash Cannonball	135
Old Home Place	94	Way Downtown	136
Old Joe Clark	95	Were You There *	137
Old Train	96	When The Golden Leaves Begin To Fall	138
Ole Slewfoot	97	When The Roll Is Called Up Yonder *	139
One Way Track	98	When The Saints Go Marching In *	140
Pallet On Your Floor	99	When The Storm Is Over	141
Panama Red	100	When You Go Walking	142
Pig In A Pen	101	Where The Soul Never Dies *	143
Poor Wayfaring Stranger *	102	Whitehouse Blues	144
Precious Memories *	103	Whither Thou Go *	145
Pretty Polly	104	Wildwood Flower	146
Rain & Snow	105	Will The Circle Be Unbroken *	147
Rank Stranger To Me *	106	Working On A Building *	148
Reuben's Train	107	Worried Man Blues	149
Rider	108	Wreck of the Old 97	150
Rocky Top	109	Guitar Chords	151
Roll In My Sweet Baby's Arms	110	Mandolin Chords	152
Roll Muddy River	111	Banjo Chords	153
Roll On Buddy	112	Other Bluegrass Products	154
Roses In The Snow	113		
Roving Gambler	114		
Salty Dog	115		
Satan's Jewel Crown *	116		
Shady Grove	117		
Silver Dagger	118		
Singing All Day & Dinner On The Ground *	119		
Sitting On Top Of The World	120		
Some Day *	121		
Sweet Sunny South	122		

* Gospel Song

About This Book

This songbook is a collection of 150 of the most popular bluegrass & gospel songs that are commonly played by bluegrass bands today. It contains melody lines to help you learn the songs, and lyrics and chord progressions in a large type on a single page to make it easy to use for jam sessions or even playing on stage. The term "fakebook" comes from jazz music meaning a book that you can use to play your way through the songs even if you aren't familiar with them.

The Keys

Most of the songs are arranged in the Key of G, since this is a very common key for bluegrass. To play in other keys, you would use a capo on the guitar, banjo, and dobro. The guitar is played in G to get the distinctive G runs that are a signature sound in bluegrass. The banjo and dobro are tuned to an open G chord so they are also played in G. You will have to transpose songs for the mandolin, fiddle, and bass since they don't use capos.

Most of the songs are arranged for a male singer. If you are a female singer, transpose them to a comfortable key. As a general rule, count up 4 steps in the musical alphabet (songs in G would transpose to songs in C for a female singer).

To use a capo, use the chord progressions as written and consult the following chart:

G Fingering		C Fingering	
Capo Position	Key	Capo Position	Key
None	G	None	C
1st Fret	G# or Ab	1st Fret	C# or Db
2nd Fret	A	2nd Fret	D
3rd Fret	A# or Bb	3rd Fret	D# or Eb
4th Fret	B	4th Fret	E
5th Fret	C	5th Fret	F

To transpose songs to other keys, consult the following chart:

Key	Common Chords						
	1	4	5	2m	3m	6m	b7
G	G	C	D	Am	Bm	Em	F
Ab	Ab	Db	Eb	Bbm	Cm	Fm	Gb
A	A	D	E	Bm	C#m	F#m	G
Bb	Bb	Eb	F	Cm	Dm	Gm	Ab
B	B	E	F#	C#m	D#m	G#m	A
C	C	F	G	Dm	Em	Am	Bb
Db	Db	Gb	Ab	Ebm	Fm	Bbm	B
D	D	G	A	Em	F#m	Bm	C
Eb	Eb	Ab	Bb	Fm	Gm	Cm	Db
E	E	A	B	F#m	G#m	C#m	D
F	F	Bb	C	Gm	Am	Dm	Eb
Gb	Gb	B	Db	Abm	Bbm	Ebm	E

The Songs

The songs have all become bluegrass standards, even though some were written for other styles of music. Numerous songs by all of the traditional bluegrass artists are included as well as several tunes by "new" bluegrass bands. There are also over 50 bluegrass gospel songs included in this book. The selection was influenced by my personal tastes as well as the copyright laws. Unfortunately, several bluegrass publishing catalogues have been bought by two major publishers and they are not issuing permission to print the songs.

I would like to thank Jim Coleman for the use of his extensive bluegrass record and CD collection and Dick Freeland of Zap Publishing for his extensive knowledge of bluegrass recordings.

Records and CDs

Each page of the book has a listing of several recorded versions of the songs, so that you can see who performed the song and obtain a recording if you like. As a general rule, these recordings are currently available on CDs. Many of the original recordings from the 40's and 50's are out of print, but all of the major bluegrass artists have CD collections or box sets that are available and I have listed these collections rather than the original recording. The source for this information is a web site that lists all currently available CDs (http://www.cddb.com).

Chord Charts

There are chord charts for guitar, mandolin, and banjo in the back of the book. These charts contain all the chords you'll need to play the songs in this book. The roman numerals indicate the fret position of chords up the neck that wouldn't fit into the diagram. If you need more help on the instruments, take a look at the last page in the book for other instructional material.

The Author

Bert Casey, the author of this book, has been a professional performer and teacher in the Atlanta area for over 25 years. Bert plays several instruments (acoustic guitar, electric guitar, bass, mandolin, banjo, and flute) and has written 6 instructional books (*Acoustic Guitar Primer, Acoustic Guitar Book 2, Electric Guitar Primer, Bass Guitar Primer, Mandolin Primer, and Flatpicking Guitar Songs*) and has made five instructional DVDs (*Introduction to Acoustic Guitar, Acoustic Guitar Part 2, Introduction to Electric Guitar, Introduction to Bass Guitar, and Introduction to Mandolin*). Bert performed several years in Atlanta and the Southeast with his bands Home Remedy and Blue Moon. Since teaming up with Geoff Hohwald in 1984, Watch & Learn, Inc. has sold over 1.5 million books, videos, and DVDs world wide and continue to develop and distribute new products for the aspiring musician.

The Songs

Instantly learn and play along with 14 songs in the *Bluegrass Fakebook*.
The *Acoustic Guitar Practice CDs* by Bert Casey is a two CD set that plays 14 popular bluegrass songs using the exact words and melodies in the *Bluegrass Fakebook*. All songs are played at three speeds along with an acoustic band (guitar, bass, mandolin, and vocals). All of the verses are sung on each speed with harmony parts where appropriate. This is a fun and valuable practice tool to get you prepared for your next jam session.

Songs include: *Tom Dooley, Going Down That Road Feeling Bad, He's Got The Whole World In His Hands, Worried Man Blues, Rolling In My Sweet Baby's Arms, Banks of the Ohio, Dark Hollow, In The Pines, Amazing Grace, Pallet On Your Floor, Way Downtown, Sittin' On Top of the World, Wabash Cannonball, Crying Holy, Little Maggie, & Nine Pound Hammer.*

2 CD Set $14.95

Ain't Gonna Work Tomorrow

Traditional

Up Tempo

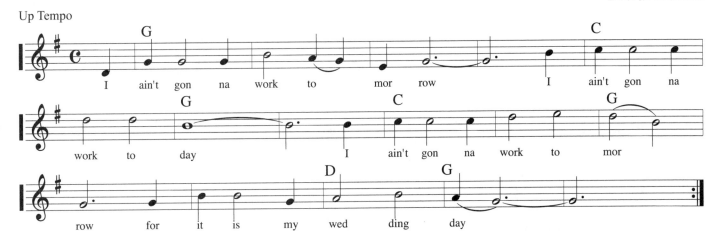

I ain't gon na work to mor row I ain't gon na
work to day I ain't gon na work to mor
row for it is my wed ding day

Chorus

I ain't gonna work tomorrow (G)
Ain't gonna work today (C) (G)
Ain't gonna work tomorrow (C) (G)
For it is my wedding day (D) (G)

I love my Mama and Papa, too
I love my Mama and Papa, too
I love my Mama and Papa, too
But I'd leave them both to go with you
Chorus

I've been all around this country
I've been all around this world
I've been all around this country, Lord
For the sake of one little girl
Chorus

I'm leaving you this lonesome song
I'm leaving you this lonesome song
I'm leaving you this lonesome song
Cause I'm gonna be gone before long
Chorus

Wilma Lee Cooper / Classic Country Favorites
Flatt & Scruggs / Flatt & Scruggs 1959 - 1963 Volume 2
Hot Rize / Radio Boogie
Leftover Salmon / Euphoria

1

All The Good Times Are Past And Gone

Traditional

Chorus

<pre>
        G   C   G
All the good times are past and gone
        G   D
All the good times are o'er
G   C   G
All the good times are past and gone
                          D   G
Little darling don't you weep no more
</pre>

I wish to the Lord I'd never been born
Or died when I was young.
I never would have seen your sparkling blue eyes
Or heard your lying tongue

Don't you see that turtle dove
That flies from pine to pine?
He's mourning for his own true love
Just like I mourn for mine.

Don't you see that passenger train
Going around the bend?
It's taking away my own true love
To never return again.

Come back, come back my own true love
And stay a while with me.
For if ever I've had a friend in this world
You've been a friend to me.

Ralph Stanley / Saturday Night and Sunday Morning
Jimmy Martin / Jimmy Martin, 1954 - 1974, Vol. 2
Ralph Stanley & the Clinch Mountain Boys / Live In Japan
Flatt & Scruggs / Flatt & Scruggs 1959 - 1963

Amazing Grace

Traditional

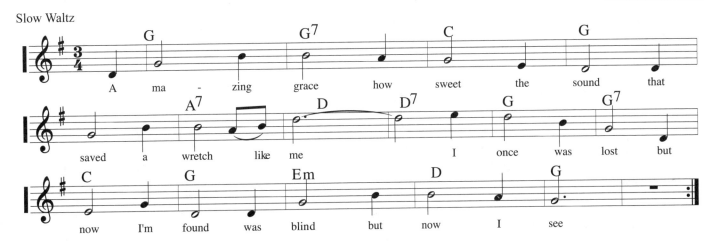

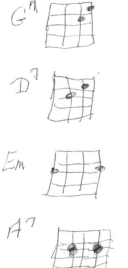

Chorus

G   G7   C   G
Amazing grace, how sweet the sound
A7   D   D7
That saved a wretch like me
G   G7   C   G
I once was lost, but now am found
Em   D   G
Was blind, but now I see

Twas grace that taught my heart to fear
And grace my fears relieved
How precious did that grace appear
The hour I first believed

Through many dangers, toils, and snares
I have already come
Tis grace hath brought me safe thus far
And grace will lead me home

When we've been here ten thousand years
Bright shining as the sun
We've no less days to sing God's praise
Than when we first begun

Seldom Scene / Baptizing
Doc Watson / Doc Watson Family
Red, White, and Blue(Grass) / Pickin' Up
Judy Collins / Amazing Grace

Angel Band

Traditional

Slow Waltz

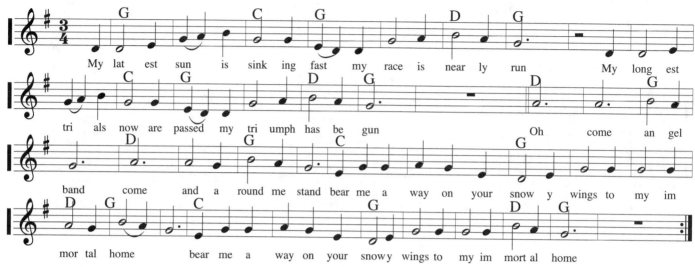

My latest sun is sinking fast
My race is nearly run
My longest trials now are passed
My triumph has begun

Chorus

Oh, come angel band
Come and around me stand
Bear me away on your snowy wings
To my immortal home
Bear me away on your snowy wings
To my immortal home

Oh, bear my loving heart to him
Who bled and died for me
Whose blood now cleanses from all sins
And gives me victory
Chorus

I've almost reached my heavenly home
My spirit loudly sings
The holy ones, behold they come
I hear the noise of wings
Chorus

Angels Rejoice

Traditional

A house not a home was a picture Satan painted
For sweet little sister and me
Our Daddy would frown while Mother was praying
His heart was so hardened that he would not believe

In anger he'd swear, his voice cold and loud
His Sundays were spent down with the gambling crowd
I've never seen my Daddy inside a house of God
For Satan held his hand down the path of sin he trod

Not long ago our circle was broken
When God called our Mother one night
In a voice sweet and low, her last words were spoken
Asking our Daddy to raise her children right

The angels rejoiced in Heaven last night
I heard my Daddy praying, "Dear God, make it right"
He was smiling and singing with tears in his eyes
While Mother with the angels rejoiced last night

While Mother with the angels rejoiced last night

Nicolette Larson / Nicolette
Harris, Emmylou / Portraits
Gram Parsons & The Flying Burrito Brothers / Sleepless Nights

Are You Washed In The Blood

Traditional

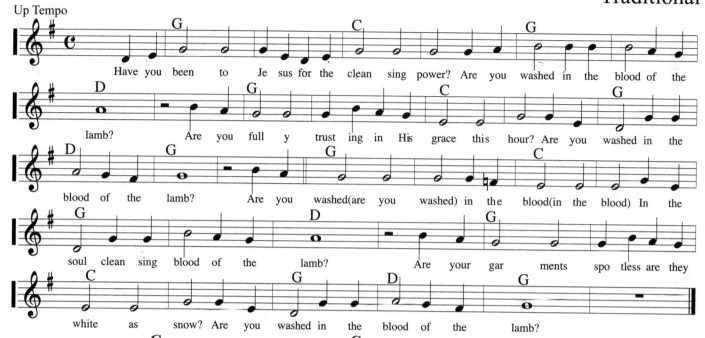

Have you been to Jesus for the cleansing power?
Are you washed in the blood of the lamb?
Are you fully trusting in His grace this hour?
Are you washed in the blood of the lamb?

Chorus

Are you washed (are you washed) in the blood (in the blood)
In the soul cleansing blood of the lamb?
Are your garments spotless are they white as snow?
Are you washed in the blood of the lamb?

Are you walking daily by the savior's side?
Are you washed in the blood of the lamb?
Do you rest each moment in the Crucified?
Are you washed in the blood of the lamb?
Chorus

Lay aside your garments that are stained with sin
And be washed in the blood of the lamb?
There's a fountain flowing for the soul unclean
Oh, be washed in the blood of the lamb
Chorus

Loretta Lynn / All Time Gospel Favorites
The Lewis Family / 20 Country Bluegrass Hits
Willie Nelson & Bobbie Nelson / Old Time Religion
Mountain Therapy / Songs From An Old Fashioned Tradition

Banks of the Ohio

Traditional

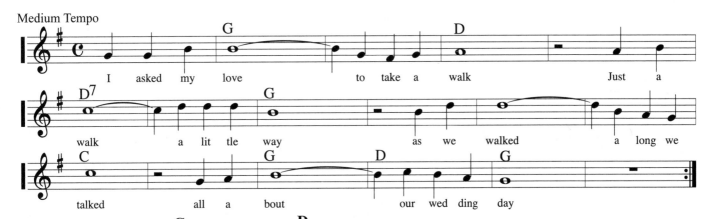

I asked my love to take a walk
Just a walk a little way
As we walked along we talked
All about our wedding day

Chorus

Only say that you'll be mine
And our home will happy be
Down beside where the waters flow
Down on the banks of the Ohio

I held a knife close to her breast
As into my arms she pressed
She cried, "Oh, Willie, don't murder me,
I'm not prepared for eternity."

I took her by her lily white hand
Led her down where the waters stand
There I pushed her in to drown
And watched her as she floated down

I started home tween twelve and one
I cried, "My God, what have I done."
I murdered the only woman I loved
Because she would not be my bride

The very next morning about half-past four
The sheriff came knocking at my door
He said, "Young man, come with me and go
Down to the banks of the Ohio"

Battle of New Orleans

Jimmy Driftwood

In 1814 we took a little trip
Along with Colonel Jackson down the mighty Mississipp
We took a little bacon and we took a little beans
And we caught the bloody British in the town of New Orleans

Chorus

We fired our guns and the British kept a coming
There wasn't nigh as many as there was a while ago
We fired once more and they began to running
Down the Mississippi to the Gulf of Mexico

We looked down the river and we seen the British come
And there must have been a hundred of them beating on the drums
They stepped so high and they made their bugles ring
We stood behind our cotton bales and didn't say a thing   Chorus

Old Hickory said we could take em by surprise
If we didn't fire a musket till we looked em in the eyes
We held our fire till we seen their faces well
We opened up our squirrel guns and really gave em, well we   Chorus

Bridge

Well, they ran through the briars and they ran through the brambles
And they ran through the bushes where the rabbits couldn't go
They ran so fast the hounds couldn't catch em
On down the Mississippi to the Gulf of Mexico

We fired our cannon till the barrel melted down
Then we grabbed an alligator and we fought another round
We filled his head with cannonballs and powdered his behind
And when we touched the powder off the gator lost his mind   Chorus

8

A Beautiful Life

Traditional

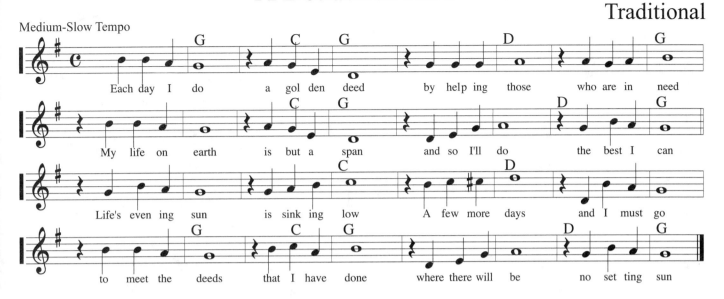

Each day I do a golden deed
By helping those who are in need
My life on earth is but a span
And so I'll do the best I can

Chorus

Life's evening sun is sinking low
A few more days and I must go
To meet the deeds that I have done
Where there will be no setting sun

To be a child of God each day
My light must shine along the way
I'll sing His praise while ages roll
And strive to help some troubled soul.

While going down life's weary road
I'll try to lift some traveler's load
I'll try to turn the night to day
Make flowers bloom along the way

The only life that will endure
Is one that's kind and good and pure
And so for God I'll take my stand
Each day I'll lend a helping hand

The Bluebirds Are Singing For Me

Lester Flatt

Up Tempo

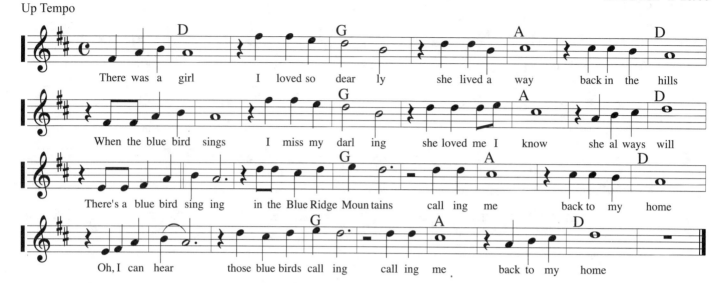

There was a girl I loved so dearly
She lived away back in the hills
When the bluebird sings I miss my darling
She loved me, I know she always will

Chorus

There's a bluebird singing (bluebird singing)
In the Blue Ridge Mountains (Blue Ridge Mountains)
Calling me back to my home
Oh, I can hear (I can hear)
Those bluebirds calling (bluebirds calling)
Calling me back to my home

When I reached my home I was oh, so lonely
The one I loved had gone away
That sad news came from her mother
She's sleeping there beneath the clay
Chorus

Now tonight I'm far from the Blue Ridge Mountains
Far from my home back in the hills
I'm going back to the Blue Ridge Mountains
These memories, they haunt me still
Chorus

Marty Stuart / Once Upon A Time
Country Gentlemen / The Best of the Early Country Gentlemen
Mac Wiseman & Lester Flatt / Lester And Mac

10

Boil Them Cabbage Down

Traditional

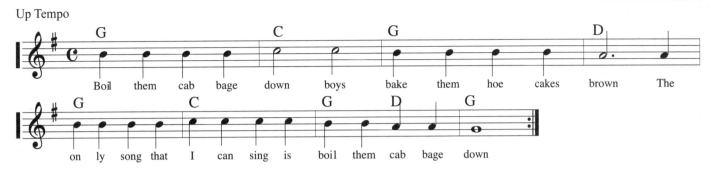

Boil them cabbage down boys bake them hoe cakes brown The

on ly song that I can sing is boil them cab bage down

Chorus

Raccoon has a bushy tail
Possum's tail is bare
Rabbit's got no tail at all
But a little bunch of hair

Boil them cabbage down boy
Bake that hoecake brown
The only song that I can sing is
Boil them cabbage down

Raccoon and the possum
Coming cross the prairie
Raccoon said to the possum
Did she want to marry
Chorus

Raccoon up a 'simmon tree
Possum on the ground
Possum say to the Raccoon
"Won't you shake them 'simmons down"?
Chorus

Jaybird died with the whooping cough
Sparrow died with the colic
Along came the frog with a fiddle on his back
Inquiring his way to the frolic
Chorus

Born To Be With You

Don Robertson

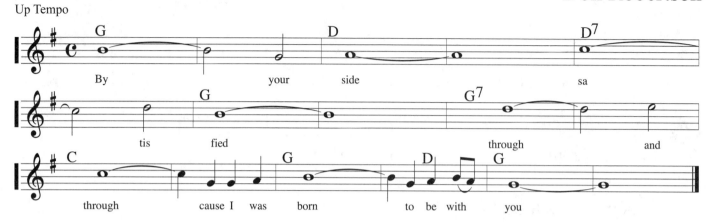

By your **side**
Satis**fied**
Through & through
Cause I was born to be with you

Wondrously
Love can see
So I knew
That I was born to be with you

Do I find
Peace of mind
Yes I do
Cause I was born to be with you

JD Crowe & The New South - Live In Japan
Louvin Brothers - Close Harmony
Jim Reeves - Welcome To My World

© 1956 Don Robertson Music Corp. (ASCAP)
© Renewed by Donald Irwin Robertson 1984
Original Publisher Edwin H. Morris & Co. Inc.
All Rights Reserved

Bound To Ride

Traditional

Up Tempo

Coming down from Tenn e see rid ing on the line Study ing bout that gal of mine

couldn't keep from crying Ho ney babe I'm bound to ride don't you want to go?

C
Coming down from Tennessee, riding on the line
D
Studying bout that gal of mine, couldn't keep from crying
G

Chorus

Honey babe I'm bound to ride
D   G
Don't you want to go?

Going to Atlanta just to look around
Things don't suit me I'll hunt another town
Chorus

Riding on a streetcar, looking o'er the town
Eating salty crackers, ten cents a pound
Chorus

Working on a railroad saving all I can
Looking for that woman that ain't got no man
Chorus

If I die a railroad man, bury me under the ties
So I can see old number nine as she goes rolling by
Chorus

See that train a coming, coming round the bend
Goodbye, my little darling, I'm on my way again
Chorus

Ralph Stanley / Bound To Ride
Emerson & Waldron / The Best of Emerson & Waldron
Jim Mills / Bound To Ride

13

Bury Me Beneath The Willows

Traditional

Up Tempo

Bury me beneath the wil lows un der the weep ing wil low tree When she hears that I am sleep ing May be then she'll think of me

Chorus

Bury me beneath the $\overset{G}{}$ $\overset{C}{}$ willows
Under the weeping willow $\overset{D}{}$ tree
When she hears that I $\overset{C}{}$ am sleeping
Maybe then she'll think of me

My heart is sad and I'm in sorrow
Weeping for the one I love
When shall I see her, oh, no never
Till we meet in Heaven above

Tomorrow was to be our wedding
But Lord, oh Lord, where can she be?
She's gone, she's gone to find another
She no longer cares for me

She told me that she did not love me
I couldn't believe it was true
Until an angel softly whispered,
"She no longer cares for you".

Place on my grave a snow white lily
To prove my love for her was true
To show the world I died of grieving
For her love I could not win

Careless Love

Traditional

Up Tempo

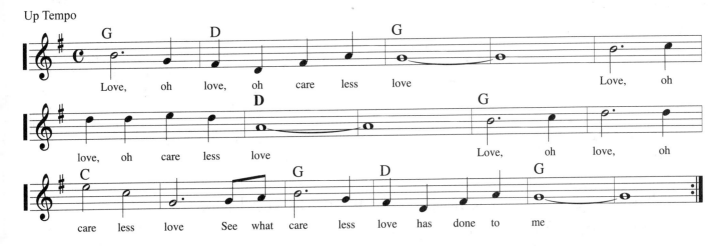

Chorus

Love, oh love, oh careless love
Love, oh love, oh careless love
Love, oh love, oh careless love
See what careless love has done to me

When my apron strings were long
When my apron strings were long
When my apron strings were long
You passed my window with a song

Now my apron strings won't tie
Now my apron strings won't tie
Now my apron strings won't tie
You pass my cabin door right by

I love my mom and daddy, too
I love my mom and daddy, too
I love my mom and daddy, too
But I'd leave them both to go with you

Children Go Where I Send Thee

Charles Love

Children go where I send thee, how shall I send thee
I'm gonna send thee one by one
One for the little bitty baby
Born, born, born in Bethlehem

Children go where I send thee, how shall I send thee
I'm gonna send thee two by two
Two for Paul & Silas, one for the little bitty Baby
Born, born, born in Bethlehem

Children go where I send thee, how shall I send thee
I'm gonna send thee three by three
Three for the Hebrew children, two for Paul & Silas
One for the little bitty baby
Born, born, born in Bethlehem

Children go where I send thee, how shall I send thee
I'm gonna send four by four
Four for the four that stood at the door, three for the Hebrew children,
Two for Paul & Silas, one for the little bitty baby
Born, born, born in Bethlehem

(Add one line for each verse)
Five for the gospel preachers
Six for the six that never got fixed
Seven for the seven that never went to heaven
Eight for the eight that stood at the gate
Nine for the nine that dressed so fine
Ten for the ten commandments

Ralph Stanley / 50th Anniversary Collection
Peter, Paul, & Mary / A Holiday Celebration

Columbus Stockade Blues

Traditional

Up Tempo

Way down in Col um bus Geor gia Wan na be
back in Ten nes see Way down in Col um bus stock ade my
friends all turned their backs on me Go and leave me if you wish
to Ne ver let it cross your mind If in your heart
you love an oth er Leave me lit tle dar ling I don't mind

Way down in Columbus, Georgia
Wanna to be back in Tennessee
Way down in Columbus stockade
My friends all turned their backs on me

Chorus

Go and leave me if you wish to
Never let it cross your mind
If in your heart you love another
Leave me, Little Darling, I don't mind

Last night as I lay sleeping
I dreamt I held you in my arms
When I awoke I was mistaken
I was peering through the bars

Many a night with you I rambled
Many an hour with you I spent
Thought I had you heart forever
Now I find it was only lent

Willie Nelson / Nashville Was The Roughest...
Norman Blake / Slow Train Through Georgia
Chesapeake / Rising Tide
Sons of the Pioneers / San Antonio Rose

Cripple Creek

Traditional

Up Tempo

Well I married my wife in the month of June Married her up by the light of the moon Wailing down on Cripple Creek We've been down there about a week Goin' down to Cripple Creek, goin' on a run Goin' down to Cripple Creek to have a little fun Goin' down to Cripple Creek to see my girl

Well I married my wife in the month of ^CJune
Married her up by the li^Dght of the ^Gmoon
^GWailing down on ^CCripple ^GCreek
We've been down there ab^Dout a ^Gweek

^GGoin' down to Cripple Creek, goin' on a run
Goin' down to Cripple Creek to h^Dave a little ^Gfun
^GGoin' down to Cripple Creek, goin' in a whirl
Goin' down to Cripple Creek to s^Dee my ^Ggirl

Now Cripple Creek girls is about half grown
Jumped on the man like a dog on a bone
Roll my britches up until my knees
Gonna cross 'ol Cripple Creek when I please
Chorus

Hey, I got a girl at the head of the creek
Goin up to see her about 2 times a week
Kiss her on the mouth, sweet as any wine
Wrap herself around me like a sweet potato vine
Chorus

Now, Cripple Creek's wide and Cripple Creek's deep
Wade old Cripple Creek before I sleep
Hills are steep and the roads are muddy
And I'm so dizzy that I can't stand steady
Chorus

Chorus

Ralph Stanley / Songs My Mother Taught Me and More
Flatt & Scruggs / Flatt & Scruggs 1959 - 1963
Jimmy Martin / Jimmy Martin -1954-1974

18

Crying Holy

Traditional

Up Tempo

Cry - ing ho ly un to the Lord   Cry - ing ho
ly un to the Lord   If I could I sure ly
would stand on that rock   where Mo ses stood

Chorus

G
Crying holy unto the Lord
C   **G**
Crying holy unto the Lord
If I could I surely would
            D   **G**
Stand on that rock where Moses stood

Sinners run and hide your face
Sinners run and hide your face
Sinners run to that rock and hide your face
The rock's dried out, no hiding place
Chorus

Lord I ain't no stranger now
Lord I ain't no stranger now
I've been introduced to the Father and the Son
And I ain't no stranger now
Chorus

JD Crowe & The New South / The New South
Country Gentlemen / Let The Light Shine Down
Bill Monroe / The Essential Bill Monroe & The Monroe Brothers

Dancing With The Angels

Peter Rowan

There's a pathway of darkness, there's a pathway of light
And they meet at the old crossroads
The angels are calling if your spirit will harken
All is forgiven, lay down your weary load

You'll be dancing (dancing), dancing (dancing), dancing with the angels
Just like old Daniel in the lion's den
The door will open and the feast spread out before you
Dancing with the angels while the lion's roar

Old Satan's dark powers are hungry for confusion
Unsatisfied ever greedy for more
If you look to your heart at the spirit there a blooming
If it's bright and shining, sin can harm you no more
Chorus

Kind angels of mercy are waiting there to greet you
Standing on the shore of everlasting light
They sing, "Come and join us across the shining waters
Our lanterns of love will guide us through the night"
Chorus

New Grass Revival / Barren County

Daniel Prayed

Traditional

I read about a man one day who wasted not his time away
He prayed to God every morning, noon, and night
He cared not for the things of hell, trusted one and never fail
Old Daniel prayed every morning, noon, and night

Chorus

Old Daniel saved his living soul while upon his journey trod
He prayed to God every morning, noon, and night
He cared not for the King's who call, trusted God's saving creed
Old Daniel prayed every morning, noon, and night

They cast him in the lion's den because he would not honor men
When he prayed to God every morning, noon, and night
Jaws were locked, it made him shout, God soon brought him safely out
Old Daniel prayed every morning, noon, and night
Chorus

Now brother let us watch and pray what Daniel did from day to day
He prayed to God every morning, noon, and night
Two can play deering do, things of God he'll take us through
Old Daniel prayed every morning, noon, and night
Chorus

Dark Hollow

Traditional

Medium Tempo

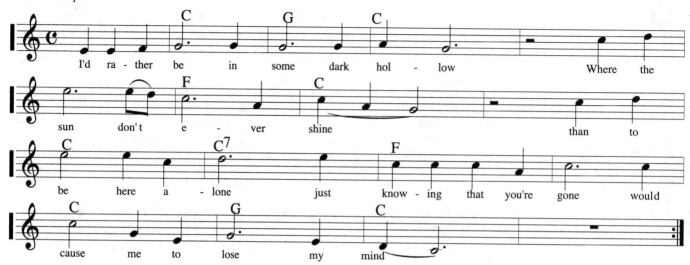

I'd rather be in some dark hollow
Where the sun don't ever shine
Than to be here alone just knowing that you're gone
Would cause me to lose my mind

So blow your whistle freight train
Carry me further on down the track
I'm going away, I'm leaving today
I'm going but I ain't coming back

I'd rather be in some dark hollow
Where the sun don't ever shine
Than to be in some big city
In a small room with your love on my mind
Chorus

I'd rather be in some dark hollow
Where the sun don't ever shine
Than to see you another man's darling
And know that you'll never be mine
Chorus

Chorus

Seldom Scene / Live At The Cellar Door
The Kentucky Colonels / Livin' In The Past
Grateful Dead / Grateful Dead - Playin' Acoustic
Muleskinner / Muleskinner

22

Darling Corey

Traditional

Medium Tempo

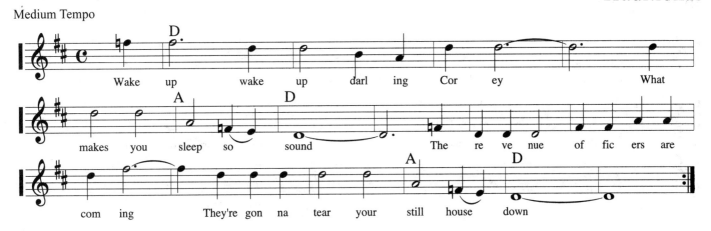

Wake up   wake   up   darl   ing   Cor   ey   What
makes   you   sleep   so   sound   The   re   ve   nue   of   fic   ers   are
com   ing   They're   gon   na   tear   your   still   house   down

Wake up, wake up darling Corey **D**
What makes you sleep so sound **A** **D**
The revenue officers are coming
They're gonna tear you still-house down **A** **D**

Well the first time I seen darling Corey
She was sitting by the banks of the sea
Had a forty-four around her body
And a five string on her knee

Go away, go away darling Corey
Quit hanging around my bed
Your liquor has ruined my body
Pretty women gone to my head

Dig a hole, dig a hole in the meadow
Dig a hole in the cold damp ground
Dig a hole, dig a hole in the meadow
We're gonna lay darling Corey down

Can't you hear them bluebirds a-singing
Don't you hear that mournful sound?
They're preaching darling Corey's funeral
In some lonesome graveyard ground

Seldom Scene / Act One
Doc Watson / The Doc Watson Family

Do Lord

Traditional

Medium Tempo

Chorus

Do Lord, oh, do Lord, oh, do remember me (G)
Do Lord, oh, do Lord, oh, do remember me (C...G)
Do Lord, oh, do Lord, oh, do remember me
From away beyond the blue (D...G)

I got a home in glory land that out shines the sun
I got a home in glory land that out shines the sun
I got a home in glory land that out shines the sun
Away beyond the blue
Chorus

Peter will be waiting with a welcome just for me
And angels songs will fill the air through all eternity
Oh, that will be a joyful everlasting jubilee
Far away beyond the blue
Chorus

The Holmes Brothers / Jubilation
Floyd Cramer / Sounds of Sunday

24

Don't This Road Look Rough And Rocky

Traditional

Medium Tempo

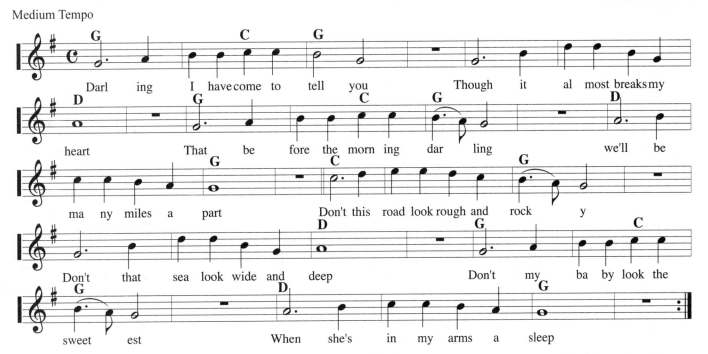

Darling, I have come to tell you
Though it almost breaks my heart
That before the morning, darling
We'll be many miles apart

Don't this road look rough and rocky
Don't that sea look wide and deep
Don't my baby look the sweetest
When she's in my arms asleep

Chorus

Don't you hear the nightbirds calling
Far across the deep blue sea?
While of others you are thinking
Won't you sometimes think of me?

One more kiss before I leave you
One more kiss before we part
You have caused me lots of trouble
Darling, you have broke my heart

Seldom Scene / Blue Ridge
Flatt & Scruggs / Songs Of Flatt & Scruggs
Osborne Brothers / Bluegrass Collection
Bluegrass Album Band / Volume 2

25

Don't Your Hear Jerusalem Moan

Traditional

Medium Tempo

Well, I got a home on the other shore
(Don't you hear Jerusalem moan)
I know I'll live there forever more
(Don't you hear Jerusalem moan)

Don't you hear Jerusalem moan?
Don't you hear Jerusalem moan?
Thank God there's a heaven and a ringing in my soul
And my soul set free, don't you hear Jerusalem moan?

It's a high road to walk and a might long way
(Don't you hear Jerusalem moan)
But your feet are just a flying when your soul is saved
(Don't you hear Jerusalem moan)
Chorus

Well, a Baptist preacher sure knows his bible
(Don't you hear Jerusalem moan)
He's on a first name basis with the Saints inside us
(Don't you hear Jerusalem moan)
Chorus

Dooley

Jayne & Dillard

Up Tempo

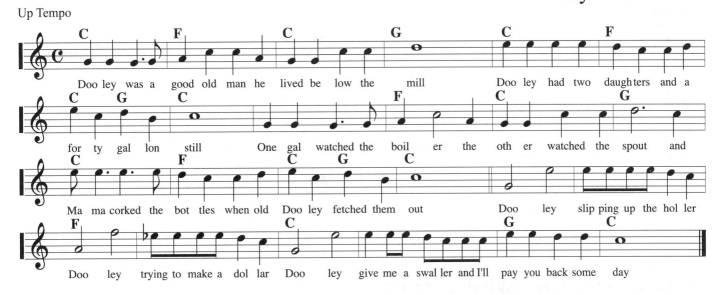

Dooley was a good old man, he lived below the mill
Dooley had two daughters & a forty gallon still
One gal watched the boiler, the other watched the spout
And Mama corked the bottles when old Dooley fetched them out

Chorus
Dooley, slipping up the holler
Dooley, trying to make a dollar
Dooley, give me a swaller & I'll pay you back some day

The revenuers came for him a slipping through the woods
Dooley kept behind them all and never lost his goods
Dooley was a trader when into town he come
Sugar by the bushel and molasses by the ton
Chorus

I remember very well the day old Dooley died
The women folk looked sorry and the men stood round and cried
Now Dooley's on the mountain, he lies there all alone
They put a jug beside him and a barrel for a stone
Chorus

© 1963 (renewed 1991)
Lansdowne Music & Winston Music Pub (ASCAP)

The Dillards / There Is A Time

Down The Road

Traditional

      G   **Em**
Down the road just a mile or two
 G   **D**   **G**
Lives a little girl named Pearly Blue
                   Em
About so high & hair is brown
 G   **D**   **G**
Prettiest thing boy in this town

Chorus

    G   **Em**
Down the road, down the road
 G   **D**   **G**
Got a little pretty girl down the road

Now any time you wanna know
Where I'm heading is down the road
See that girl on the line
You'll find me there most any old time

Now every day and Sunday, too
I go to see my Pearly Blue
Before you hear the rooster crow
You'll see me headed down the road

Clemny Rakestraw owns a farm
From the hog wash to the barn
From the barn to the rail
Made his living by carrying the mail

Now every time I get the blues
I walk the soles right off my shoes

Drifting Too Far From The Shore

Traditional

Slow Waltz

Out on the perilous deep
Where danger silently creeps
And storm so violently sweeping
You're drifting too far from the shore

Chorus

Drifting too far from the shore
You're drifting too far from the shore
Come to Jesus today, let him show you the way
You're drifting too far from the shore

Today the tempest rose high
And clouds o'er shadow the sky
Sure death is hovering nigh
You're drifting too far from the shore
Chorus

Dry Run Creek

Larry McPeak

Thirteen hundred died that day
It took ten good men just to dig the graves
They buried them shallow, they buried them deep
They buried them next to Dry Run Creek

Chorus

And their Mamas cried
Oh my Lord how their Mamas cried

Well, they weren't just blue and they weren't just grey
Death took no sides when it came that day
They laid them down side by each
They placed no stones at the head or feet
Chorus

When the digging was through they gathered round
A lonesome dove made the only sound
They said their prayers right to their feet
They left their friends at Dry Run Creek

War had been over for about a week
Word hadn't gotten to Dry Run Creek
They fought and died right to the end
Battle that should have never been
Chorus

Seldom Scene / Dream Scene

East Virginia Blues

Ralph Stanley

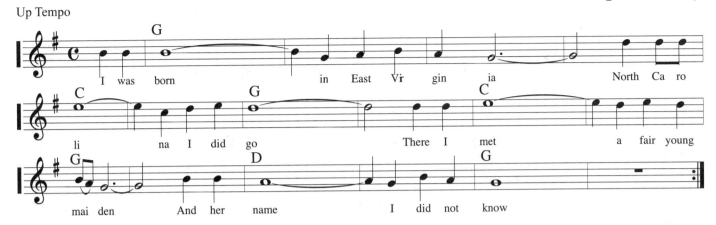

I was born in East Virginia
G

North Carolina I did go
C   G

There I met a fair young maiden
C   G

& her name I did not know
D   G

Oh her hair was dark & curly
& her cheeks were rosy red
On her breast she wore white lilies
Where I longed to lay my head

I don't want your green back dollar
I don't want your watch & chain
All I want is your heart darling
Say you'll take me back again

The ocean's deep & I can't wade in
& I have no wings to fly
I'll just get me a blue eyed boat man
For to row me over the tide

I'll go back to East Virginia
North Carolina ain't my home
I'll go back to East Virginia
Leave them North Carolineans alone

Every Time You Say Goodbye

John Pennell

Look at the sky ba by, what do you see? Looks like the tears that I cry Fall ing down like rain on the ground Ev ery time you say good bye There's a rest less feel ing knock ing at my door to day There's a sha dow hang ing round my gar den gate I read be tween the lines of words you can't dis guise Love has gone a way put these tears in my eyes

E   B7   A   B7
Look at the sky baby, what do you see?
A   B7   C#m   B7
Looks like the tears that I cry
A   B7   E   A
Falling down like rain on the ground
E   B7   E
Every time you say goodbye

Take a look around now, why don't you feel
The way that cold wind stings and bites
And your word just are like arrows through my heart
Every time you say goodbye

Chorus

        B7   A   E
There's a restless feeling knocking at my door today
        B7   E
There's a shadow hanging round my garden gate
G#
I read between the lines of words you can't disguise C#m
          F#   B7   F#m .B7
Love has gone away, put these tears in my eyes

Look at the sky baby, see how it cries
Ain't it just like my tears
Falling down like rain on the ground
Every time you day goodbye
Chorus

Fair And Tender Ladies

Traditional

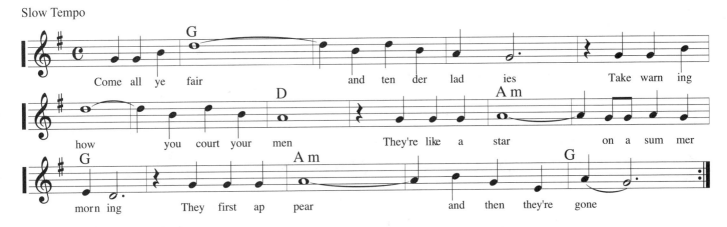

Slow Tempo

Come all ye fair and ten der lad ies Take warn ing
how you court your men They're like a star on a sum mer
morn ing They first ap pear and then they're gone

Come all ye fair and tender ladies (G)
Take warning how you court your men (D)
They're like a star (Am) on a summer morning (G)
They first appear (Am) and then they're gone (G)

They'll tell to you some loving story
And they'll make you think that they love you well
And away they'll go and court some other
And leave you there in grief to dwell

I wish I was on some tall mountain
Where the ivy rocks were black as ink
I'd write a letter to my false true lover
Whose cheeks are like the morning pink

I wish I was a little sparrow
And I had wings to fly so high
I'd fly to the arms of my false true lover
And when he'd ask, I would deny

Oh love is handsome, love is charming
And love is pretty while it's new
But love grows cold as love grows old
And fades away like morning dew

Find Me Out On A Mountain Top

Tim Stafford

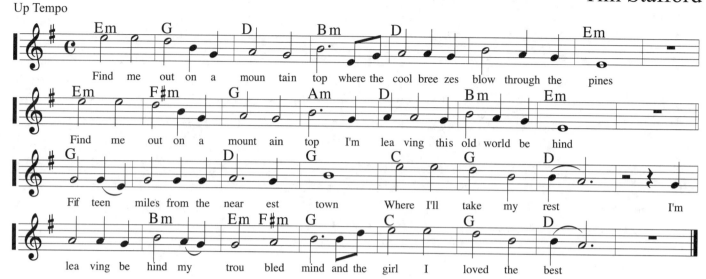

Chorus

Find me out on a mountain top
(Em) *(G)* *(D)* *(Bm)*
Where the cool breezes blow through the pines
(D) *(Em)*
Find me out on a mountain top
(Em) *(F#m)* *(G)* *(Am)*
I'm leaving this old world behind
(D) *(Bm)* *(Em)*

Fifteen miles from the nearest town
(G) *(D)* *(G)*
Where I'll take my rest
(C) *(G)* *(D)*
I'm leaving behind my troubled mind
(D) *(Bm)* *(Em)* *(F#m)* *(G)*
And the girl I loved the best
(C) *(G)* *(D)*
Chorus

A country boy in a city world
Will never find a home
Like a morning dove on a high roof top
I'm better left all alone
Chorus

34

Foggy Mountain Top

Traditional

Chorus

If I was on some Foggy Mountain top
I'd sail away to the West
I'd sail all around this whole wide world
To the girl I love the best

If I'd have listened to what Mama said
I would not be in here today
Lying around this old jailhouse
Just wasting my poor life away
Chorus

Oh, she caused me to weep, she caused me to mourn
She caused me to leave my home
Oh, the lonesome pines and the good old times
I'm on my way back home
Chorus

Flatt & Scruggs / On Foggy Mountain
The Bluegrass Band / Once Again From The Top

Footprints In The Snow

Traditional

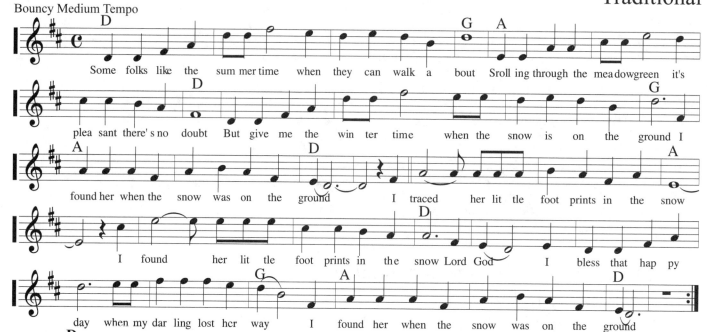

Some folks like the summer time
When they can walk about
Strolling through the meadow green,
There's comfort there no doubt
But give me the winter time
When snow is on the ground
I found her when the snow is on the ground

Chorus

I traced her little foot prints in the snow
I found her little footprints in the snow
Bless that happy day, when my darling lost her way
I found her when the snow lay on the ground

I went out to see her, there was a big round moon
Her mother said she just stepped out but would be returning soon
I found her little footprints & traced them through the snow
I found her when the snow lay on the ground

Now she's up in Heaven with that angel band
I know I'm going to meet her in that promised land
Every time the snow falls it brings back memories
I found her when the snow lay on the ground

Freeborn Man

Allison & Lindsay

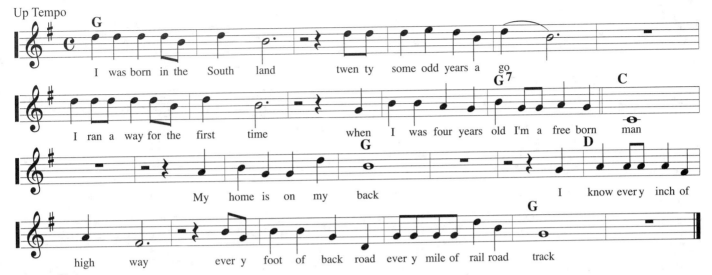

I was born in the South land   twen ty some odd years a go
I ran a way for the first   time   when I was four years old I'm a free born man
My home is on my back   I know every inch of
high way   every foot of back road every mile of rail road track

Chorus

I ^Gwas born in the Southland
Twenty some odd years ago
I ran away for the first time
When I was only four years^{G7} old

I'm a freeborn m^Can
My home is on my b^Gack
I k^Dnow every inch of highway
Every foot of back road, every mile of railroad tr^Gack

I picked oranges down in Florida, I picked cotton in Alabam'
I picked walnuts up in Oregon, I pick guitar when I can
Chorus

Got a gal in Cincinnati, got a woman in San Anton'
Always loved the girl next door, but any place is home
Chorus

Well I got this worn out guitar I carry in an old tote sack
I hocked it about 200 times, but I always get it back
Chorus

You may not like my appearance, you may not like my song
You may not like the way I sing, but you'll like the way I'm gone
Chorus

Tony Rice / Guitar
Junior Brown / 12 Shades of Brown
Jimmy Martin / Jimmy Martin - 1954 - 1974, Vol. 4

37

Friend Of The Devil

Garcia, Dawson, Hunter

I lit **G** out from Reno I was trailed **C** by 20 hounds
Didn't **G** get to sleep last night till the **C** morning came around

Chorus
Set **D** out running but I take my time a friend **Am** of the devil is a friend of mine
If I **D** get home before daylight, I just **Am** might get some sleep tonight **D**

I ran into the devil, babe, he loaned me 20 bills
Spent the night in Utah in a cave up in the hills
Chorus

I ran down to the levee but the devil caught me there
He took my $20 bill & vanished in the air
Chorus

Bridge
Got **D** two reasons why I cry away each lonely night
The first **C** one's named sweet Ann Marie
And she's my heart's delight
The second **D** one is prison, babe, & the sheriff's on **D** my trail
& if he **Am** catches up with me, I spend my life in jail **D**

Got a wife in Chino, babe, and one in Cherokee
First one says she's got my child, but it don't look like me
Chorus

38

Grateful Dead / American Beauty

Get In Line Brother

John Duffey

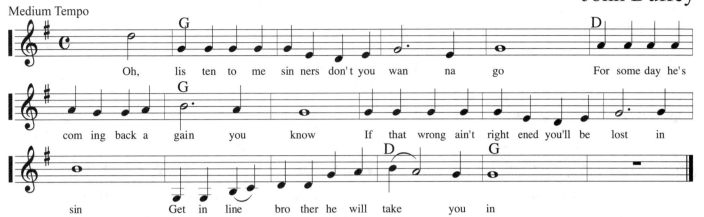

Oh, listen to me sinners don't you want to go
For some day he's coming back again you know
If that wrong ain't rightened you'll be lost in sin
Get in line brother, he will take you in

Chorus
Get in line brother if you wanna go home
Get on your knees and righten that wrong
Then you'll be singing this old time song
Get in line brother if you wanna go home

If I could tell you brother just how I feel
Then I'm sure you'd know the love of God is real
Then you'll be praying while I sing this song
Get in line brother if you wanna go home
Chorus

Now listen to me Satan I have rightened that wrong
Got a one way ticket and I'm going home
I've got no worries as I sing this song
Get in line brother if you wanna go home
Chorus

Flatt & Scruggs / Don't Get Above Your Raisin'
Legacy / A Tribute to the First Generation of Bluegrass
Johnny Cash / Johnny Cash & Friends
Seldom Scene / Baptizing

39

Ginseng Sullivan

Norman Blake

About three miles from the battail yard from the reverse curve on down
Not far south of the town depot, Sullivan's shack was found
Back on the higher ground
You could see him every day, walking down the line
With an old brown sack across his back & his long hair down behind
Speaking his worried mind

It's a long way to the Delta, from the North Georgia hills
& a tote sack full of ginseng won't pay no traveling bills
& I'm too old to ride the rail or thumb the road alone
I guess I'll never make it back to home
My muddy water Mississippi Delta home

Now the winters here they get too cold, so damp it makes me ill
Can't dig no roots in the mountain side, the ground's froze hard & still
You gotta wait at the foot of the hill
By next Summer things turn right, the company's will pay high
I'll make enough money to pay my bills & bid these mountains goodbye
Then he said with a sigh
Chorus

40

Norman Blake / Slow Train Through Georgia
The Tony Rice Unit / Manzanita

Glendale Train

J. Dawson

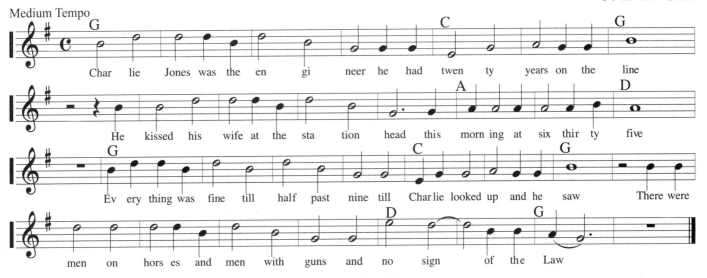

G
Charlie Jones was the engineer, he had 20 **C** years on the line **G**
He kissed his wife at the station head this **A** morning at six thirty fi**D**ve
G
Everything went fine till half past nine, till Cha**C**rlie looked up & he sa**G**w
There were men on horses & men with guns & **D**no sign of the La**G**w

Somebody robbed the Glendale Train this **C** morning at half past **G** nine
Some body robbed the Glendale Train, I **A** swear I ain't ly**D**ing
They **G** made clean off with 16 G's and two boys lying **C** cold
Somebody robbed the Glendale Train & they **D** made off with the **G** gold

Amos White was the baggage man & he clearly loved his job
Company rewarded him with a gold watch & fob
Amos he was making time when the door blew off his cord
They found Amos White in 15 pieces, 15 miles apart
Chorus

God Moves In A Wind Storm

Traditional

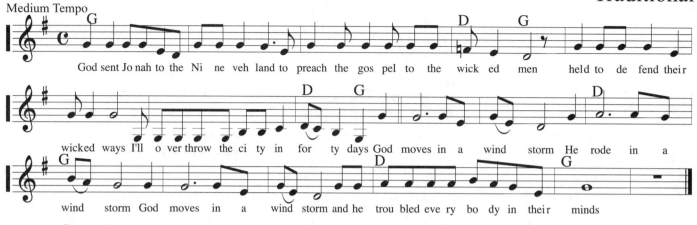

God sent Jonah to the Nineveh land to preach the gospel to the wicked men held to defend their wicked ways I'll overthrow the city in forty days God moves in a wind storm He rode in a wind storm God moves in a wind storm and he troubled everybody in their minds

G
God sent Jonah to the Nineveh land
D   **G**
To preach the gospel to the wicked men
Held to defend their wicked ways
D   **G**
I'll overthrow the city in forty days

Chorus

God moves in a wind storm
D   **G**
He rode in a wind storm
God moves in a wind storm
D   **G**
And he troubled everybody in their mind

God sent Jonah to the sea shore to make up his mind which way to go
Boarded the ship and he paid his fare
Got God angry with Jonah down there
Chorus

Jonah went down from the side of man, called on Jesus to be his friend
Disobeyed God and he had to pray
Lord sent a storm on the water that day
Chorus

Cast poor Jonah overboard, God sent a whale & swallowed him whole
Went on down to the Nineveh land
Laid poor Jonah on a bed of sand
Chorus

Jonah rose up from the land, went on walking to the Nineveh land
Preached the gospel at his command
Repent, repent you wicked men
Chorus

42

Going Down That Road Feeling Bad

Traditional

Up Tempo

G
Go - ing down that road feel - ing bad

C ... **G**
Go - ing down that road feel - ing bad

C ... **G**
Go - ing down that road feel - ing bad Lord Lord And I

D ... **G**
ain't gon - na be treat - ed this a way

Chorus

Go͡ing down that road feeling bad — **G**
Ba͡d luck's all I ever ha͡d — **C G**
Go͡ing down that road feeling ba͡d, Lord, Lord — **C G**
And I a͡in't gonna be treated this a wa͡y — **D G**

Got me way down in jail on my knees
This jailer, he sure is hard to please

Feed me on corn bread and peas, Lord, Lord
And I ain't gonna be treated this a way

Sweet mama won't buy me no shoes
She's left with these lonesome jail house blues

My sweet Mama won't buy me no shoes, Lord, Lord
And I ain't gonna be treated this a way

These two dollar shoes they hurt my feet
The jailer won't give me enough to eat

These two dollar shoes they hurt my feet, Lord, Lord
And I ain't gonna be treated this a way

I'm going where the climate suits my clothes
I'm going where these chilly winds don't blow

I'm going where the climate suits my clothes, Lord, Lord
And I ain't gonna be treated this a way

Grateful Dead - 1973-06-10 RFK Stadium
Doc Watson - The Essential Doc Watson
Johnny Cash - The Survivors Live

Gone At Last

Paul Simon

The **C** night was black, the roads were icy
Snow was **F** falling, drifts were high **C**
I was weary from my driving **Am**
When I **C** stopped to **G** rest for awhile **C**
I sat down at a truck stop
I was thinking about my past
I've had a long streak of that bad luck
But I pray it's gone at last

Chorus

C Gone at last (echo), gone at last (echo)
Gone at **F** last (echo), gone at **C** last (echo)
I've had a long streak of that bad **Am** luck
But I **C** pray it's **G** gone at **C** last
F Ooh... **C** **G** **C**

I ain't dumb, I've kicked around some, I don't fall too easily
But that boy looked so dejected, he just grabbed my sympathy
Sweet little son, what's your problem, tell me why you're so downcast
I've had a long streak of that bad luck, but I pray it's gone at last.
Chorus

Paul Simon / Born At The Right Time: The Best Of Paul Simon

A Good Woman's Love

Cy Coben

I was a rover on land and on sea
Till a good woman's love made a new man of me

Life had no meaning, it was so incomplete
Till a good woman's love put me back on my feet

Stead of roaming, I go home in the evening
She's waiting there
And I know that no matter what happens
She'll always care

And when the night falls and the moon shines above
I'm a man with a dream and a good woman's love
Bridge

Last Verse

Bridge

Goodnight, Irene

Ledbetter & Lomax

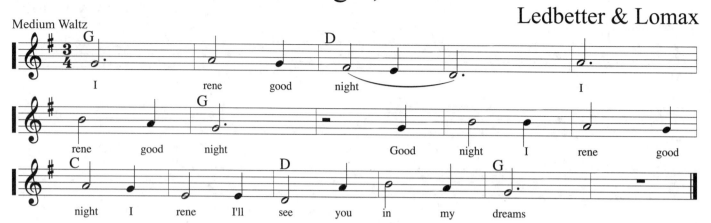

Chorus

Irene, goodnight, Irene, goodnight
Goodnight, Irene, goodnight, Irene
I'll see you in my dreams

Last Saturday night I got married
Me and my wife settled down
Now me and my wife are parted
I'm gonna take another stroll downtown
Chorus

Sometimes I live in the country
Sometimes I live in the town
Sometimes I have a great notion
To jump into the river and drown
Chorus

Stop rambling, and stop your gambling
Stop staying out late at night
Go home to your wife and your family
Sit down by the fireside bright
Chorus

TRO © 1936 (Renewed) 1950 (Renewed)
Ludlow Music Inc., NY, NY (BMI)
International Copyright Secured   Made in USA
All Rights Reserved Including Public Performance For Profit
Used by Permission

Leadbelly / Goodnight Irene
Jim Reeves / The Definitive Jim Reeves
Johnny Cash / The Man In Black 1954-1958

46

Green Pastures

Traditional

Up Tempo Waltz

Troubles and trials often betray those
Out in the weary body to stray
But we shall walk beside the still waters
With the Good Shepherd leading The Way

Those who have strayed were sought by The Master
He who once gave His life for the sheep
Out on the mountain still He is searching
Bringing them in forever to keep

Going up home to live in green pastures
Where we shall live and die never more
Even The Lord will be in that number
When we shall reach that heavenly Shore

We will not heed the voice of the stranger
For he would lead us to despair
Following on with Jesus our saviour
We shall all reach that country so fairs
Repeat 3rd Verse

47

Hallelujah I'm Ready

Traditional

Up Tempo

Chorus

Hallelujah (I am ready) I am ready (hallelujah)
I can hear the voices singing soft and low
Hallelujah (I am ready) I am ready (hallelujah)
Hallelujah I'm ready to go

In the darkness of night not a star was in sight
On a highway that leads down below
But Jesus came in and saved my soul from sin
Hallelujah I'm ready to go
Chorus

Sinners don't wait until it's too late
He's a wonderful Saviour you know
Well I fell on my knees and he answered my pleas
Hallelujah (I'm ready) I'm ready (hallelujah)
Chorus

48

He Said If I Be Lifted Up

Pace & Stamps

Down in the valley while on my knees
I asked my Jesus, "Help me please"
He promised that he'd take care of me
If I would lift him up

He said if I (he said if I), be lifted up (be lifted up)
He said if I (he said if I), be lifted up (be lifted up)
I'll be your Father, I'll be your Mother
I'll be your sister and your brother
He said if I (he said if I), be lifted up (be lifted up)
I'll bring joy (joy, joy) to your soul

When I am lonely, when I am sad
My Jesus comes and makes me glad
He is the dearest friend that I've had
And I want to lift him up
Chorus

IIIrd Tyme Out / Live At The MAC
The Kentucky Colonels / Livin' In The Past
Stanley Brothers / Hymns & Sacred Songs

He Will Set Your Fields On Fire

Traditional

There's a call that rings from the throne it springs to those have gone astray
Saying, "Come ye men and your load of sin there at the altar lay".
You don't seem to heed for the chain of greed still crushes your desires
Be assured my friend if you still offend, He will set you fields on fire

Chorus
If you don't from sin retire, He will set your fields on fire
You have heard Jesus call and in death your soul must fall
But my friend if you desire, you may join the Heavenly Choir
And rejoice with Him free from every sin when He sets this world on fire

You have heard His voice, seen the soul rejoice that trusted in His grace
You have blushed with sin as He knocked within but still you hide your face
From the blessed Lord & His own true word but still you say retire
Leave the downward path, kindle not his wrath, or He'll set your fields on fire

Take a friend's advice, make the sacrifice, completely turn from sin
Taking up the cross, counting earth as dross, let Jesus live within
When Temptations come keep on facing home to Satan never hire
But rejoice and pray on the last great day when He sets this world on fire

Country Gentlemen / One Wide River To Cross
Bill Monroe / A Voice From On High

50

He's Got The Whole World

Traditional

He's got the whole world in His hands,
C
He's got the whole world in His hands,
G
He's got the whole world in His hands,
C
He's got the whole world in His hands.
G   C

He's got my brothers and my sisters in His hands,
He's got my brothers and my sisters in His hands,
He's got my brothers and my sisters in His hands,
He's got the whole world in His hands.

He's got the sun and the rain in His hands,
He's got the moon and the stars in His hands,
He's got the wind and the clouds in His hands,
He's got the whole world in His hands.

He's got the rivers and the mountains in His hands,
He's got the oceans and the seas in His hands,
He's got you and he's got me in His hands,
He's got the whole world in His hands.

He's got everybody here in His hands,
He's got everybody there in His hands,
He's got everybody everywhere in His hands,
He's got the whole world in His hands.

High On A Mountain

Owen Chapman

Medium Tempo

As I look at the valleys down below
They were green just as far as I could see
As my memories returned oh, how my heart did yearn
For you and the days that used to be

Chorus

High on a mountain the wind blowing free
Thinking about the days that used to be
High on a mountain standing all alone
Wondering where the years of my life had flown

Oh, I wonder if you ever think of me
Or if time has blotted out your memory
As I listen to the breeze whisper gently through the trees
I'll always cherish what you meant to me
Chorus

Del McCoury Band / Blue Side Of Town

Hobo Song

Jack Bonus

Too late to feel sorrow, too late to feel pain
He's just an old hobo, lost out in the rain
He'll never cause trouble, so don't have no fear
He's just an old hobo, & he'll soon be far away from here

Chorus

He used to be a gambling man just like you
Until he sank so low there was nothing no one could do
Repeat

Oh don't make him ask you, oh don't make him beg
He was a war hero & that's how he lost his leg
He killed 30 Indians with one cannon ball
He's just an old hobo, asleep out in the hall
Chorus

A wife & 5 children who live in LA
How they miss their dear Daddy, who's gone so far away
Well they still have his picture, it's hung up on the wall
Now he's just an old hobo, asleep out in the hall
Chorus

53

Hot Corn, Cold Corn

Traditional

Up Tempo

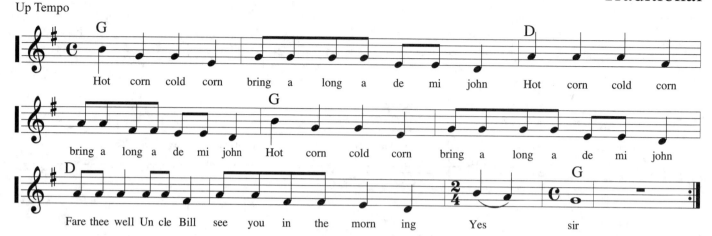

Chorus

$\overset{G}{H}$ot corn, cold corn, bring along a demijohn
$\overset{D}{H}$ot corn, cold corn, bring along a demijohn
$\overset{G}{H}$ot corn, cold corn, bring along a demijohn
$\overset{D}{F}$are thee well, Uncle Bill, see you in the morning , Yes $\overset{G}{s}$ir

Upstairs, downstairs, down in the kitchen
Upstairs, downstairs, down in the kitchen
Upstairs, downstairs, down in the kitchen
See Uncle Bill, he's a raring and pitching, Yes sir
Chorus

Old Aunt Peggy won't you fill em up again
Old Aunt Peggy won't you fill em up again
Old Aunt Peggy won't you fill em up again
Ain't had a drink since I don't know when, yes sir
Chorus

Yonder comes the preacher and the children are a crying
Yonder comes the preacher and the children are a crying
Yonder comes the preacher and the children are a crying
Chickens are a hollering, toenails are a flying, yes sir
Chorus

I Ain't Broke (But I'm Badly Bent)

Traditional

Medium Tempo

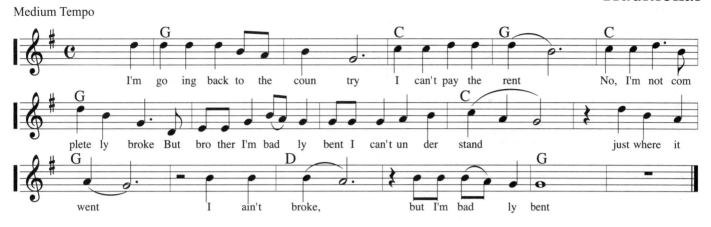

I'm ^Ggoing back to the country
I ^Ccan't pay the ^Grent
No, I'm not com^Cpletely ^Gbroke
But brother I'm badly bent
I can't under^Cstand just where it ^Gwent
I ain't ^Dbroke, but I'm badly ^Gbent

Well, I had a lot of money
But to the city I went
I met this really good looking girl
And that's where my money went
Now I know just where it went
I ain't broke, but I'm badly bent

When I get back to the country
I'll be living in a tent
Ma and Pa will sure be mad
At all the money I spent
They won't understand just where it went
I ain't broke, but I'm badly bent

Now everybody knows just where it went
Well, I ain't broke, but brother I'm badly bent

I Am A Pilgrim

Traditional

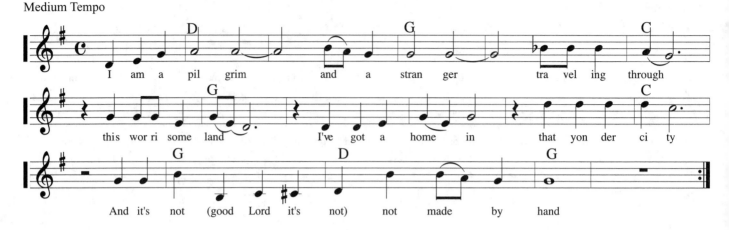

Chorus

I am a pilgrim and a stranger
Traveling through this worrisome land
I've got a home in that yonder city
And it's not (Good Lord it's not), not made by hand

I've got a mother, a sister, and a brother
Who have gone on before
And I'm determined to go and meet them, Good Lord
Over on that other shore
Chorus

I'm going down to the river of Jordan
Just to cleanse my weary soul
If I could touch but the hem of his garment, Good Lord
I do believe it would make me whole
Chorus

The Nitty Gritty Dirt Band / Will The Circle Be Unbroken
Kentucky Colonels / Living In The Past
Country Gentlemen / The Early Rebel Recordings

I Never Will Marry

Traditional

They say that love's a gentle thing
But it's only brought me pain
For the only girl I ever lost
Has gone on the morning train

Chorus

I never will marry
I'll take me no wife
I expect to live single
All the days of my life

The train pulled out and the whistle blew
With a long and a lonesome mourn
She's gone, she's gone like the morning dew
And left me all alone

Well there's many a change in the winter wind
And a change in the clouds design
There's many a change in a young girl's heart
But never a change in mine

I'll Fly Away

Albert E. Brumley

G
Some glad morning, when this life is over
C   G
I'll fly away
To a home on God's celestial shore
D   G
I'll fly away

 Chorus

I'll (fly away) fly away, Oh glory
C
I'll (fly away) fly away (in the morning) **G**
When I die Hallelujah, by and by
D   G
I'll (fly away) fly away (I'll fly away)

When the shadows of this life have grown
I'll fly away
Like a bird from prison bars have flown
I'll fly away
Chorus

Just a few more weary days and then
I'll fly away
To a land where joys shall never end
I'll fly away
Chorus

58

I'll Remember You, Love, In My Prayers

Traditional

Medium Tempo

When the cur tains of night are pinned back by the stars And the beau ti ful

moon sweeps the sky Dew drops from hea ven are kiss ing the

rose It's then that my mem o ry flies

When the **G** curtains of night are pinned back by the stars
And the beautiful moon sweeps the sky **C**
G Dewdrops from heaven are kissing the rose **F**
It's then **G** that my **D** memory flies **G**

Well, upon the wings of a beautiful dove
I'll hasten this message of cheer
And I'll bring you a kiss of affection and say
I'll remember you, love, in my prayers

Now the angels of Heaven are guarding the good
As God has ordained them to do
In answer to prayers that I offer to him
I know there's one waiting for you

Now go where you will upon land or on sea
And I'll share all your sorrows and cares
At night as I kneel by my bedside to pray
I'll remember you, love, in my prayers

Well, at night as I kneel by my bedside to pray
I'll remember you, love, in my prayers

If I Lose

Tami LaRue

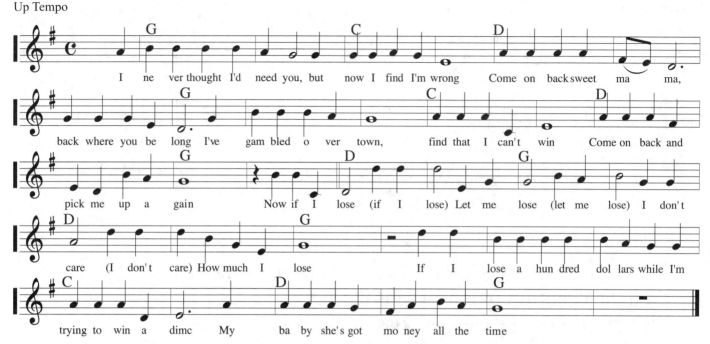

I never thought I'd need you, but now I find I'm wrong _(G ... C)_
Come on back sweet mama, back where you belong _(D ... G)_
I've gambled over town, find that I can't win _(C)_
Come on back and pick me up again _(D ... G)_

Chorus

Now if I lose (if I lose) _(D)_
Let me lose (let me lose) _(G)_
I don't care (I don't care) _(D)_
How much I lose _(G)_
If I lose a hundred dollars while I'm trying to win a dime _(C)_
My baby, she's got money all the time _(D ... G)_

Of all the other gals I know, none can take your place
Cause when I get into a jam, they just ain't in the race
So now that you're back, let's make another round
With you here by my side, babe, the deal just can't go down

Ralph Stanley and Friends / Clinch Mountain Country
Ricky Skaggs / Bluegrass Rules

In The Pines

Traditional

Chorus

In the pines, in the pines
Where the sun never shines
And you shiver when the cold winds blow
Ooh, ooh, ooh, ooh, ooh, ooh
Ooh, ooh, ooh

The longest train I ever saw
Went down that Georgia Line
The engine passed at six o'clock
And the cab passed by at nine
Chorus

Little girl, little girl, what have I done
That makes you treat me so
You've caused me to weep, you've caused me to mourn
You've caused me to leave my home
Chorus

I asked my captain for the time of day
He said he throwed his watch away
It's a long steel rail and a short cross tie
I'm on my way back home

Bill Monroe & the Blue Grass Boys / In The Pines
Jimmy Martin / Sunny Side of the Mountain
Osborne Brothers / Up This Hill and Down
Boone Creek / One Way Track

61

It Won't Work This Time

Aubrey Holt

Walked in yesterday and you told me you'd be leaving
Left a note said, "Mama won't be back"
But you'll come back again and I've got news for you dear
You won't have a home and that's a fact

Chorus

Don't you come back on your knees asking my forgiveness
Pack your bags and move on down the line
Don't you roll them eyes at me, telling me you're sorry
It's too late babe and it won't work this time

I've always been around, Lord when you needed someone
I played the role till I knew each line by heart
But now it's time to change, won't you find another playmate
Someone who'll be glad to play the part
Chorus

Alison Krauss / Every Time You Say Goodbye

Jacob's Vision

Traditional

Chorus

Hallelu**G**jah to Jesus who died on the tree
To raise up this ladder of **D**mercy for **G**me
Press onward, climb upward, the top is in view
There's a crown of bright glory a**D**waiting for **G**you

As Jacob was traveling, was weary one day
While at night on a stone for a pillow did lay
A vision appeared of a ladder so high
It stood on the earth while the top reached the sky
Chorus

This ladder is tall and yet so well made
Stood thousands of years and never decayed
High winds from the heavens they reel and they rock
But the angels they guard it from bottom to top
Chorus

Jesse James

Traditional

Up Tempo

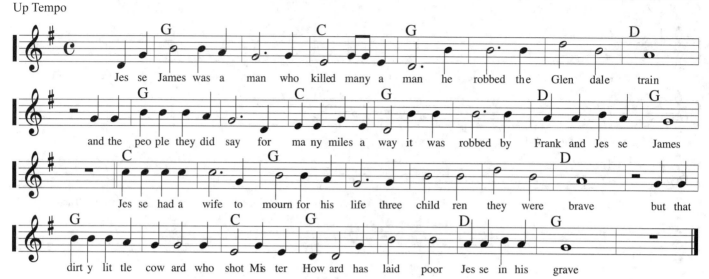

Jesse James was a man who killed many a man
G   C   G

Jesse James was a man who killed many a man
He robbed the Glendale train
And the people they did say for many miles away
It was robbed by Frank and Jesse James

Jesse had a wife to mourn for his life
Three children they were brave
But that dirty little coward who shot Mr. Howard
Has laid poor Jesse in his grave

It was on a Wednesday night, the moon was shining bright, they robbed the Glendale train
And the people they did say for many miles away, it was robbed by Frank and Jesse James
Chorus

It was on a Saturday night when Jesse was at home, talking with his family brave
Robert Ford came along like a thief in the night and laid poor Jesse in his grave
Chorus

Robert Ford, that dirty little coward, I wonder how he feels
For he ate of Jesse's bread and he slept in Jesse's bed and he laid poor Jesse in his grave
Chorus

This song was made by Billy Gashade as soon as the news did arrive
He said there was no man with the law in his hand who could take Jesse James when alive
Chorus

64

John Hardy

Traditional

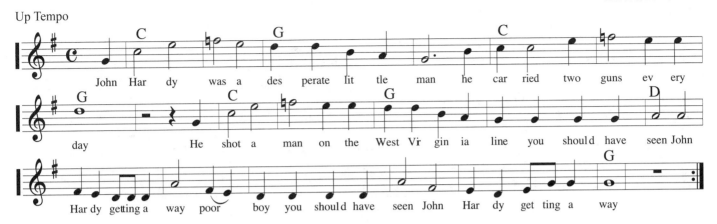

Up Tempo

John Hardy was a desperate little man he carried two guns every day He shot a man on the West Virginia line you should have seen John Hardy getting a way poor boy you should have seen John Hardy getting a way

John Hardy was a desperate little man
He carried two guns every day
He shot a man on the West Virginia line
You should have seen John Hardy getting away, poor boy
You should have seen John Hardy gettin away

He went on across to the East Stone bridge
There he thought he'd be free
Up steps the sheriff and he takes him by the arm
Saying, "Johnny, come along with me, poor boy,
Johnny, come along with me".

He sent for his Mama and his Papa, too
To come and go his bail
But there weren't no bail on a murder charge
So they threw John Hardy back in jail, poor boy
Threw John Hardy back in jail

John Hardy had a pretty little girl
The dress that she wore was blue
She came into the jailhouse hall
Saying, "Johnny, I'll be true to you, poor boy,
Johnny, I'll be true to you".

I've been to the East and I've been to the West
Traveled this wide world around
Been to the river and I've been baptized
And now I'm on my hanging ground
Now I'm on my hanging ground

Lily Brothers / Folkways
Tony Rice / Guitar

65

John Henry

Up Tempo

John Henry was a little baby boy, you could hold him in the palm of your hand

His Papa cried out this lonesome farewell, saying,

"Johnny gonna be a steel driving man, Lord, Lord, Johnny gonna be a steel driving man".

John Henry went upon the mountain, his hammer was striking fire
But the mountain was too tall, John Henry was too small
So he laid down his hammer and he died, Lord, Lord, laid down his hammer and he died

John Henry went into the tunnel, had his captain by his side
The last words that John Henry said,
"Bring a cool drink of water before I die, Lord, Lord, cool drink of water before I die".

Talk about John Henry as much as you please, say & do all that you can
There never was born in the United States never such a steel driving man, Lord, Lord,
Never such a steel driving man

John Henry had a little woman and her name was Polly Ann
John Henry took sick and he had to go to bed
Polly drove steel like a man, Lord, Lord, Polly drove steel like a man

John Henry told his captain, I want to go to bed
Lord, fix me a pallet, I want to lay down
Got a mighty roaring in my head, Lord, Lord, mighty roaring in my head

Took John Henry to the graveyard & they buried him under the sand

Now every locomotive comes a roaring by

Says, "Yonder lies a steel driving man, Lord, Lord, yonder lies a steel driving man".

Jordan

Traditional

Medium Tempo

Oh listen as you tread life's journey take Jesus as your daily guide (A)
Tho you may feel pure and safely without Him walking by your side (B7) (E)
When you come to make the crossing at the end of your pilgrim's way (A)
If you ever will meet our Savior you'll surely meet Him on that day (E) (A)

Chorus

Now look at that cold Jordan, look at these deep waters (E) (A)
Look at that wide river, oh hear the mighty billows roar (D) (E) (A)
You'd better take Jesus with you, He's a true companion (E) (A)
For I'm sure without Him that you never will make it o'er (D) (E) (A)

That awful Day of Judgement is coming in the by and by
We'll see out Lord descending in Glory from on high
So let us keep in touch with Jesus & in his grace the Love of God
That we may be ever called ready when He calls us over Jordan's Tide
Chorus

67

Katy Daley

Ralph Stanley

Chorus

Come on down the mountain, Katy Daley (G)
Come on down the mountain, Katy do (D)
Can't you hear us calling, Katy Daley
We want to drink your good old mountain dew (G)

With her old man she came from Tampararay
In the pioneer days of '42
Her old man was shot in Tombstone City
For the making of his good old mountain dew
Chorus

Wake up and pay attention Katy Daley
I am the judge that's gonna sentence you
All the boys at court has drunk the whiskey
And tell the truth, I drink a little, too
Chorus

So to the jail they took poor Katy Daley
And very soon the gates were opened wide
Angels came to court Katy Daley
Took her far across the Great Divide
Chorus

Kneel Down And Pray Up

Bill Castle

Up Tempo

$$G$$
If you are a sinner and you are astray
$$C \qquad G$$
If ever you stumble along the way
$$A7 \qquad D$$
My friend, old Satan, he's using you
$$G \qquad C \qquad G$$
But listen and I'll tell you what you'd better do
$$D \qquad G$$

Chorus

$$G$$
Well, you better kneel down (you better kneel down)
$$C \qquad G$$
And you better pray up (and you better pray up)
$$A7 \qquad D$$
Cause the road up ahead friends sometimes is rough
Better live your life (better live your life)
$$C \qquad G$$
In the light of his love (in the light of this love)
And you better kneel down (you better kneel down)
$$D \qquad G$$
And you better pray up

If you're heavy laden and lonely at heart
If the road you're traveling is cold and dark
If you need a friend to walk along with you
Well, listen and I'll tell you what you'd better do
Chorus

69

Lou Reid, Terry Baucom & Carolina / Carolina Moon

Knockin' On Your Door

Traditional

Chorus

I'm knockin' on your door again my darling
I'm knockin' on your door please answer me
Well, I've tried to make you realize my darlin'
That no one else was ever meant for me

I remember dear you said you'd always love me
And you promised me a happiness so true
But now you've gone away dear with another
And I wonder if you feel the way I do
Chorus

I never read the letter that you wrote my little darlin'
I'm sailing far across the deep blue sea
I'm knockin' on your door again my darling
To return the letters that you wrote to me
Chorus

So goodbye my dear I know you'll soon forget me
And I hope you find happiness so true
But whenever you make your sweet heart remember
That no one else will be the same for you
Chorus

Last Train From Poor Valley

Norman Blake

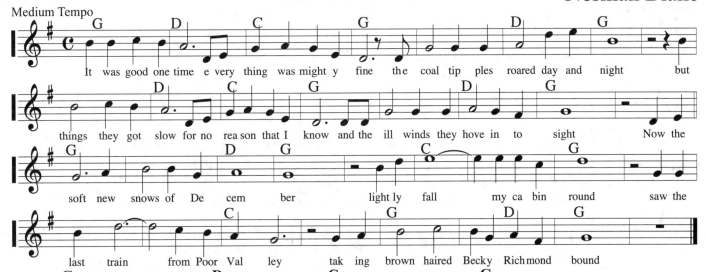

It was good one time, everything was mighty fine
The coal tipples roared day and night
But things got slow for no reason that I know
And the ill winds they hove into sight

Well, the mines all shut down, everybody layed around
There wasn't very much that you could do
'Cept stand in that line, get your ration script on time
And woman I could see it killing you

Now the soft new snows of December
Lightly fall my cabin round
Saw the last train from Poor Valley
Taking brown haired Becky Richmond bound

It's been coming on, I knew you would soon be gone
For leaving crossed your mind every day
And then you said to me, "Things are bad at home, you see
I guess I'd better be on my way"
Chorus

I should blame you now, though I never could somehow
A miner's wife you weren't cut out to be
It wasn't what you thought, just dreams that you bought
When you left home and ran away with me
Chorus

Chesapeake / Full Sail
Norman Blake / Fields Of November
Seldom Scene / Act Two

71

The Legend Of The Rebel Soldier

Charlie Moore

In a dreary Yankee prison where a Rebel soldier lay
By his side there stood a preacher ere his soul should pass away
And he faintly whispered, "Parson," as he clutched him by the hand
"Oh Parson, tell me quickly will my soul pass through the Southland?"

"Will my soul pass through the Southland, through old Virginia grand
Will I see the hills of Georgia & the green fields of Alabam?
Will I see that little church house where I pledged my heart and hand
Oh, Parson, tell me quickly, will my soul pass through the Southland

Was for loving dear old Dixie in this dreary cell I lie
Was for loving dear old Dixie in this northern state I die
Will you see my little daughter will you make her understand
Oh, Parson, tell me quickly, will my soul pass through the Southland?
Then the Rebel Soldier died.

Life Is Like A Mountain Railway

Traditional

Life is like a mountain railway with an engineer that's brave
We must make the run successful from the cradle to the grave
Watch the hills, the curves, and tunnels never falter, never fail
Keep your hands upon the throttle and your eyes upon the rail

Blessed saviour thou wilt guide us
Till we reach that blissful shore
Where the angels come to join us
In God's grace forever more

As you roll across the trestle spanning Jordan's swelling tide
You behold the Union depot into which your train will glide
There you'll meet the superintendent God the Father, God the Son
With a hearty, joyous plaudit weary pilgrim welcome home

Chorus

The Seldom Scene / Act Four
Bill Monroe / I Saw The Light
Amazing Rhythm Aces / Third Rate Romance
Nitty Gritty Dirt Band / Will The Circle Be Unbroken 2

73

Like A Train

Traditional

Up Tempo

I was a loner, Lord I didn't care
Where my next home was, I knew not where
I had nobody for to call my friend
I'll not pass this way again

Chorus

Like a train that's rolling down the railroad
Like a train that's rolling down the track
I'm leaving here to find my destination
I'm leaving here, ain't never coming back

I had a sweetheart down in El Paso
Thought that she would love me so
She went and left me for someone else
Left me here all by myself
Chorus

I lay here thinking, Lord of where to go
What I run into, I'll never know
There's nothing for me in this old town
Maybe someday I'll settle down
Chorus

Little Bessie

Traditional

Medium Tempo

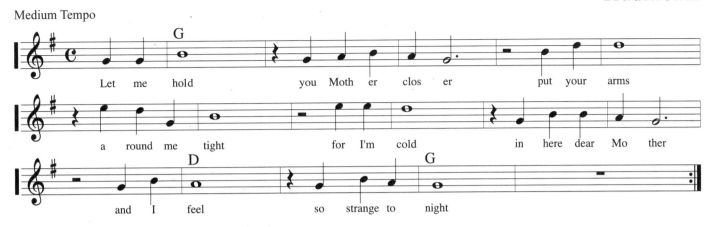

G
Let me hold you Mother closer put your arms around me tight
For I'm cold in here dear Mother and I feel **D** so strange tonight **G**

Something hurts me oh dear Mother like a stone upon my breast
Can I wonder, Mother, wonder why it is I cannot rest

On the day while you were working as I lay upon my bed
I was trying to be patient and remember what you said

Just before the lamps were lighted, just before the children came
While the moon was very quiet, I heard someone call my name

Come up here, my little Bessie, come up here and live with me
Where little children never suffer through the long eternity

In the silent hour of midnight, in the silence, calm and deep
Lying in her Mother's bosom, Little Bessie fell asleep

Now up yonder past the portals that are shining very far
Little Bessie now is tended by her saviour's love and care

Country Gentlemen / The Award Winning Country Gentlemen
JD Crowe / Bluegrass Holiday
Red, White and Blue (Grass) / Very Popular
Ricky Skaggs / Ancient Tones

Little Maggie

Traditional

Up Tempo

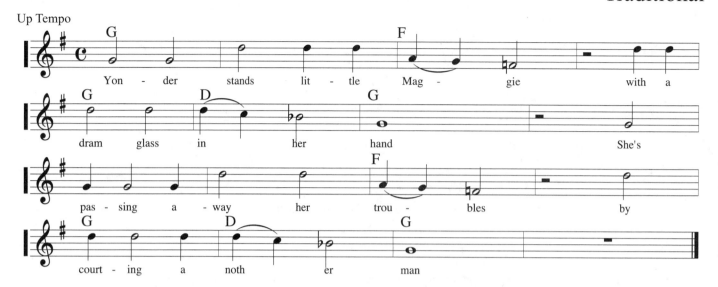

Yonder stands little Maggie with a dram glass in her hand
She's passing away her troubles by courting another man

Oh how can I ever stand it just to see them two blue eyes
Shining in the moonlight like two diamonds in the skies

Pretty flowers were made for blooming, pretty stars were made to shine
Pretty women were made for loving, Little Maggie was.made for mine

Last time I saw little Maggie she was setting on the banks of the sea
With a forty-four around her and a banjo on her knee

Lay down your last gold dollar, lay down your gold watch and chain
Little Maggie's gonna dance for Daddy, listen to this old banjo ring

I'm going down to the station with my suitcase in my hand
I'm going away for to leave you, I'm going to some far distant land

Go away, go away little Maggie, go and do the best you can
I'll get me another woman, you can get you another man

Ralph Stanley / Ralph Stanley Plays Requests
Bill Monroe / Bluegrass Ramble
Ricky Skaggs / Bluegrass Rules

Little White Church

Traditional

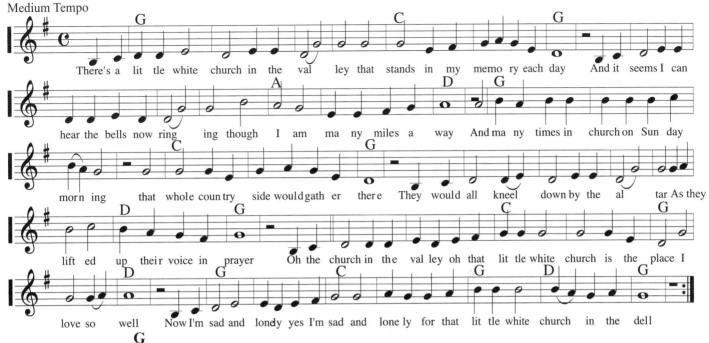

There's a little white church in the valley
That stands in my memory each day
And it seems I can hear the bells now ringing
Though I am many miles away
And many times in church on Sunday morning
That whole countryside would gather there
They would all kneel down by the altar
As they lifted up their voices in prayer

Chorus

Oh, the church in the valley, oh, that little white church
Is the place I love so well
Now I'm sad and lonely, yes I'm sad and lonely
For that little white church in the dell

They would sing the old song Rock of Ages
Oh Christ, let me hide myself in thee
And I know some of them are now waiting
Just o'er the dark and stormy sea.
I know that troubles all are ended
And happy forever they will be.
They are waiting and watching up yonder
For the coming home of you and me
Chorus

Long Journey Home

Traditional

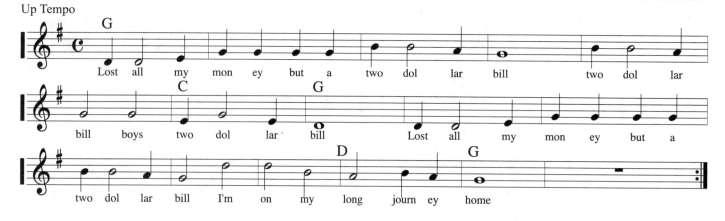

Chorus

Lost all my money but a two dollar bill
Two dollar bill, boys, two dollar bill
Lost all my money but a two dollar bill
I'm on my long journey home

Cloudy in the West and it looks like rain
Looks like rain, boys, looks like rain
Cloudy in the west and it looks like rain
I'm on my long journey home
Chorus

Black smoke a rising and it surely is a train
Surely is a train, boys, surely is a train
Black smoke arising and it sure looks like rain
I'm on my long journey home
Chorus

Starting into raining and I've got to go home
Got to go home, boys, got to go home
Starting into raining and I've got to go home
I'm on my long journey home
Chorus

Kentucky Colonels / Long Journey Home
The Stanley Brothers / Long Journey Home
J.D. Crowe & The New South / Flashback

78

Lord, I'm Coming Home

Traditional

Slow Waltz

I wandered far away from God now I'm coming home
the path of sin too long I've trod Lord, I'm coming home
Coming home coming home ne ver more to roam
o pen wide thine arms of love Lord I'm coming home

  G   **C** **G**   **D**
I wandered far away from God now I'm coming home
 G   **C** **G**   **D** **G**
The path of sin too long I've trod, Lord, I'm coming home

Chorus
     C   **G**   **D**
Coming home, coming home, never more to roam
G   **C** **G**   **D** **G**
Open wide thine arms of love, Lord, I'm coming home

I've wasted many precious years, now I'm coming home
I now repent with bitter tears, Lord, I'm coming home

I'm tired of sin and straying, Lord, now I'm coming home
I'll trust Thy love, believe Thy word, Lord, I'm coming home

My soul is sick, my heart is sore, now I'm coming home
My strength renew, my hope restore, Lord, I'm coming home

My only hope, my only plea, now I'm coming home
That Jesus died, and died for me, Lord, I'm coming home

I need His cleansing blood I know, now I'm coming home
Oh wash me whiter than the snow, Lord, I'm coming home

Jimmy Martin / Jimmy Martin, 1954 - 1974, Vol. 2
Country Gentlemen / The Early Rebel Recordings
The Lewis Family / 20 Country Bluegrass Hits

Lost & I'll Never Find The Way

Traditional

Up Tempo

Lonesome, lonesome
Pining away
Now you said it's best we part even though it breaks my heart
I'm lost and I'll never find the way

Since you said we must part, darling you broke my heart
I'm drifting like a ship lost at sea
In a world of despair it is so lonesome there
Dear, why don't you come back to me
Chorus

Now you said you'd be true, no one else would ever do
I believed in you with all my heart and soul
But you broke every vow and it's all over now
I'm left in this world alone and cold
Chorus

80

Mama Don't 'Low

Traditional

Chorus

Mama don't 'low no banjo playing round here
Mama don't 'low no banjo playing round here
Well, I don't care what mama don't 'low
Gonna play my banjo anyhow
Mama don't 'low no banjo playing round here

Mama don't 'low no guitar playing round here
Mama don't 'low no guitar playing round here
Well, I don't care what mama don't 'low
Gonna play my guitar anyhow
Mama don't 'low no guitar playing round here

Mama don't 'low no talking round here
Mama don't 'low no talking round here
Well, I don't care what mama don't 'low
Gonna shoot my mouth off anyhow
Mama don't 'low no talking round here

Mama don't 'low no singing round here
Mama don't 'low no singing round here
Well, I don't care what mama don't 'low
Gonna sing my head off anyhow
Mama don't 'low no singing round here

Man Of Constant Sorrow

Tami LaRue

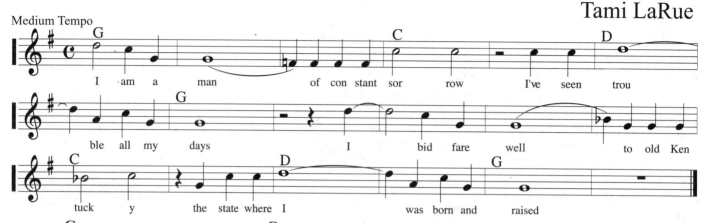

I am a man of constant sorrow
I've seen trouble all my days
I bid farewell to old Kentucky
The state where I was born and raised

For six longs years I've been in trouble
No pleasure here on earth I find
For in this world I'm bound to ramble
I have no friends to help me now

It's fare thee well my own true lover
I never expect to see you again
For I'm bound to ride that northern railroad
Perhaps I'll die upon this train

You can bury me in some deep valley
For many years where I may lay
Then you may learn to love another
While I am sleeping in my grave

It's fare you well to a native country
The places I have loved so well
For I have seen all kinds of trouble
In this cruel world, no tongue can tell

Maybe your friends think I'm just a stranger
My face you'll never see no more
But there is one promise that is given
I'll meet you on God's golden shore

The Stanley Brothers / Clinch Mountain Bluegrass
Joan Baez / Where Have All The Flowers Gone
Blue Highway / Troubles Up and Down the Road

82

Memories Of Mother And Dad

Albert Price

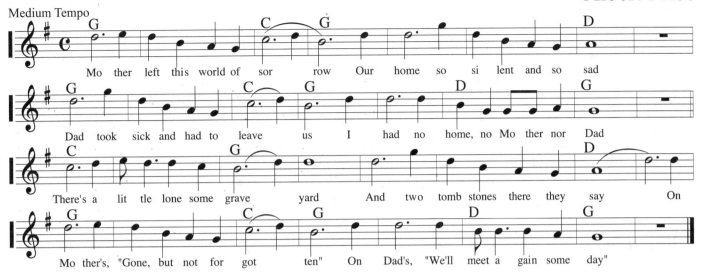

Mo ther left this world of sor row Our home so si lent and so sad

Dad took sick and had to leave us I had no home, no Mo ther nor Dad

There's a lit tle lone some grave yard And two tomb stones there they say On

Mo ther's, "Gone, but not for got ten" On Dad's, "We'll meet a gain some day"

G   C   G
Mother left this world of sorrow
                   D
Our home so silent and so sad
G   C   G
Dad took sick and had to leave us
    D   G
I had no home, no Mother nor Dad

Chorus

   C   G
There's a little lonesome graveyard
                     D
And two tombstones there they say
G   C   G
On Mother's, "Gone, but not forgotten"
     D   G
On Dad's, "We'll meet again some day"

I'd often go out to the graveyard
Where they laid them down to rest
I can almost hear him whisper
Trust in God, He'll do the rest
Chorus

Their souls have gone up to heaven
Where they rest with God above
There they'll meet with friends and loved ones
And share with all his precious love
Chorus

Ricky Skaggs & Tony Rice / Skaggs & Rice
Bill Monroe / The Music of Bill Monroe 1952-1959

83

Methodist Pie

Traditional

Up Tempo

Went down to camp meeting just the other afternoon for to hear 'em dance and sing
Telling each other how to love one another and make hallelujahs ring
Old Uncle Dan'l and Brother Ebenezer and Rufus and Singing Gal Sue
& Paulie & Melinda & old Brother Billy, well I never seen a happier crew

Chorus

Oh, children (oh, children) I believe (I believe)
Oh, children (oh, children) I believe (I believe)
Oh, children (oh, children) I believe (I believe)
I'm a Methodist till I die
I'm a Methodist, Methodist till I believe, I'm a Methodist till I die
When old grim death come a knocking at my door, I'm a Methodist till I die

Now they all go there to have some fun and eat their grub so fine
Have apple sauce butter & sugar in the gourd & a great big Methodist pie
You oughta hear 'em ringing when they all get to singing that good old Bye & Bye
Brother Jimmy McGee in the top of a tree hollered Lord I was born to die

Now they all join hands, dancing round a ring, keep singing all the while
You'd think it was cyclone coming through the air you can hear 'em shout half a mile
Then the bell rings loud & the great big crowd breaks ranks & up they fly
While I pour on the sugar in the gourd and clean up the Methodist pie

Midnight Flyer

Paul Craft

Chorus

Ooh, midnight flyer
Engineer won't you let that whistle moan
Ooh, midnight flyer
Paid my dues and I feel like traveling on

A runaway team of horses ain't enough to make me stay
So throw your rope on another man and pull him down your way
Make him into someone who can take the place of me
Make him any kind of cool you wanted me to be
Chorus

Maybe I'll go to Sante Fe, maybe San Anton'
Any town is where I'm bound, any way to get me gone
Don't think about me, never let me cross your mind
Cept when you hear that midnight, lonesome whistle whine
Chorus

Midnight On The Stormy Deep

Traditional

Slow Tempo

Was mid night on   the storm y deep   My so li

ta   ry watch I keep   But to think of her   I left be

hind   and asked if she'd   be true and kind

Was midnight on the stormy deep
D   **A**   **D**
My solitary watch I keep
But to think of her I left behind
G   **D**
And asked if she'd be true and kind
A   **D**

I never shall forget the day, that I was forced to go away
In silence there my head she'd rest and hold me to her loving breast

Oh Willie, don't go back to sea, there's other girls as good as me
But none can love you true as I, pray don't go where the bullets fly

The deep, deep sea may us divide and I may be some other's bride
But still my thoughts will sometimes stray to thee when thou art far
away

I never have proved false to thee, the heart I gave was true as thine
But you have proved untrue to me, I can no longer call thee mine

Then fare thee well, I'd rather make my home upon some icy lake
Where the southern sun refuse to shine, than to trust a love so false as
thine

Doc Watson / Riding The Midnight Train
Bill Monroe / Country Music Hall of Fame Series
The Tony Rice Unit / Manzanita

Midnight Train

Traditional

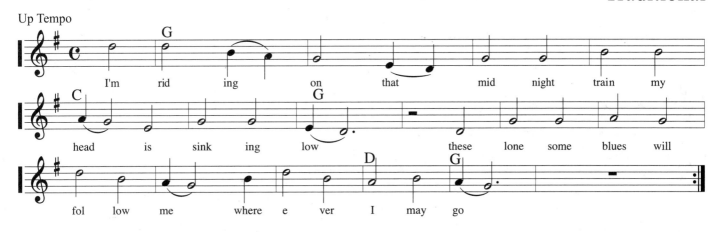

Up Tempo

I'm riding on that midnight train my head is sinking low these lonesome blues will follow me where ever I may go

Chorus

I'm riding on that midnight train
My head is sinking low
These lonesome blues will follow me
Where ever I may go

No matter what I say or do
You're never satisfied
I tried and tried so many times
I'm leaving you now goodbye
Chorus

Oh, why on Earth was I ever born
I'll never understand
To fall in love with a woman like you
In love with another man
Chorus

Milwaukee Here I Come

Lee Fikes

Milwaukee is where we were before we came here
Working in a brewery, making the finest beer
She came to me on a pay day night said, "Let's go to Tennessee"
So we came down to Nashville to the Grand Old Opry

Chorus

I'm gonna get on the old turnpike and I'm gonna ride
I'm gonna leave this town till you decide
Which one you want the most, them Opry stars or me
Milwaukee, here I come, from Nashville, Tennessee

We turned on the TV, Minnie Pearl was talking loud
I said, "That's the woman for me, I love her there's no doubt
I'm leaving here right now to find out where she's at
If I can't get her then I'll settle for little pretty Tammy Wynette"
Chorus

I'm going downtown and trade my old Ford for an Olds
I might get all drunked up and trade it for a Rolls
One thing I know for sure, I'll always be blue
There ain't no way to get drunk enough to stop my loving you
Chorus

George Jones / 24 Greatest Hits
Jimmy Martin / Jimmy Martin - 1954 - 1974

Model Church

Traditional

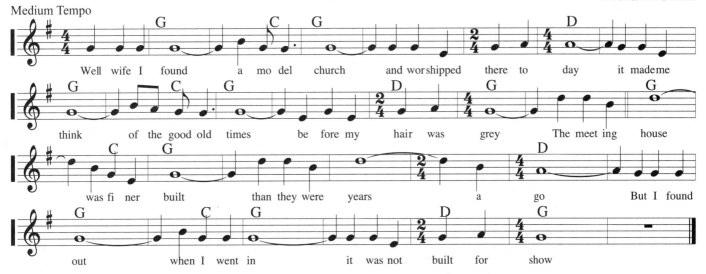

Well, wife I found a model church and worshipped there today
It made me think of the good old times before my hair was grey
The meeting house was finer built than they were years ago
But I found out when I went in, it was not built for show

The sexton did not set me down away back by the door
He knew that I was old and ill and saw that I was poor
He must have been a Christian man, he led me boldly through
The long aisle of that crowded church to find a pleasant view

I wish you'd heard the singing choir, it had the old time ring
The preacher said with trumpet voice, "Let all the people sing".
Old Correlation was the tune, the music upward rose
I thought I heard the angel choir strike on their harps of gold

I tell you wife it did me good to sing those hymns once more
I felt just like some wrecked Marine who gets a glimpse of shore
It made me want to lay aside this weather beaten boat
And anchor in that blessed port, forever from the storm

Dear wife the toil will soon be o'er, the victory soon be won
But a shining strand is just ahead, our race is nearly run
We're nearing Canaan's happy shore, our hopes are bright and fair
Thank God we'll never sin again, there'll be no sorrow there
There'll be no sorrow there
In heaven above where all in love
There'll be no sorrow there

Moonlight Midnight

Peter Rowan

If you ever feel lonesome ^{A... superscript} and you're down in San Antone
Just beg steal or borrow two nickels or a dime
And call me on the phone
I'll meet you at Alamo Mission and we can say our prayers
The Holy Ghost and the Virgin Mother will heal us
As we kneel there

In the moonlight, in the midnight
In the moonlight, midnight moonlight
In the moonlight, in the midnight
In the moonlight, midnight moonlight

If you ever feel sorrow for the deeds you have done
With no hope for tomorrow in the setting of the sun
The ocean is howling with things that might have been
And that last good morning sunrise
Will be the brightest you've ever seen
Chorus

Chorus

90

Old & In The Way / Old & In The Way
New Riders Of The Purple Saga / Midnight Moonlight

My Home's Across The Smoky Mountains

Traditional

Up Tempo

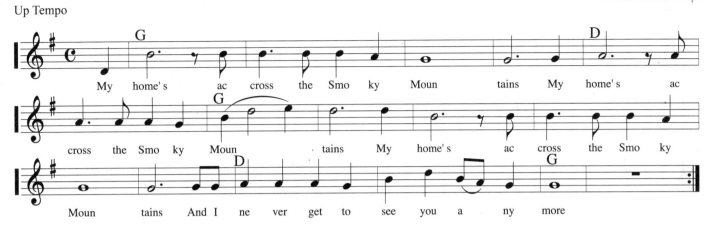

My home's across the Smoky Mountains My home's ac
cross the Smoky Moun tains My home's ac cross the Smo ky
Moun tains And I ne ver get to see you a ny more

Chorus

G
My home's across the Smoky Mountains
D   G
My home's across the Smoky Mountains
My home's across the Smoky Mountains
      D   G
And I never get to see you any more

Goodbye my little Sugar Darling
Goodbyc my little Sugar Darling
Goodbye my little Sugar Darling
And I never get to see you any more

Rock my baby, feed it candy
Rock my baby, feed it candy
Rock my baby, feed it candy
And I never get to see you any more

My home's across the Smoky Mountains
My home's across the Smoky Mountains
My home's across the Smoky Mountains
And I never get to see you any more

New River Train

Traditional

Up Tempo

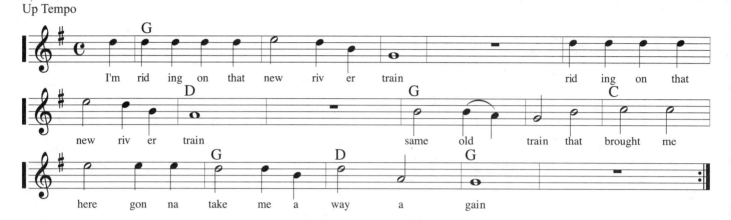

I'm rid ing on that new riv er train   rid ing on that
new riv er train   same old train that brought me
here gon na take me a way a gain

Chorus

I'm riding on that new river train <small>G</small>
Riding on that new river train <small>D</small>
Same old train that brought me here <small>G   C</small>
Gonna take me away again <small>G   D   G</small>

Darling, you can't love one
Darling, you can't love one
You can't love one and have any fun
Darling, you can't love one
Chorus

Darling, you can't love two
Darling, you can't love two
You can't love two and still be true
Darling, you can't love two
Chorus

(three) You can't love three and still love me
(four) You can't love four and love any more
(five) You can't love five and get money from my hive
(six)   You can't love six, for that kind of love don't mix

Norman Blake & Tony Rice / Blake & Rice
Doc Watson / Old Timey Concert
Bill Monroe / The Essential Bill Monroe & The Monroe Brothers

92

Nine Pound Hammer

Traditional

This nine pound hammer is a little too heavy
For my size, buddy for my size
Roll on buddy, don't you roll so slow
How can I roll when the wheels won't go

It's a long way to Harlan, and a long way to Hazard
Just to get a little booze, just to get a little booze

Oh, the nine pound hammer killed John Henry
Ain't gonna kill me, ain't gonna kill me

There ain't one hammer down in this tunnel
That can ring like mine, that can ring like mine
Rings like silver, shines like gold
Rings like silver, shines like gold

Buddy when I'm long gone, won't you make my tombstone
Out of number nine coal, out of number nine coal

I'm going on the mountain, just to see my baby
And I ain't coming back, no I ain't coming back.

Flatt & Scruggs / Flatt & Scruggs 1959 - 1963
Merle Travis / Songs of the Coal Mines
The Nitty Gritty Dirt Band / Will The Circle Be Unbroken
Tony Rice / Guitar

Old Home Place

Webb & Jayne

It's been ten long years since I left my home
In the hollow where I was born
Where the cool fall nights make the wood smoke rise
And the fox hunter blows his horn

I fell in love with a girl from the town
I thought that she would be true
Then I ran away to Charlottesville
And worked in a sawmill, too

Chorus

What have they done to the old home place
Why did they tear it down
And why did I leave my plow in the field
And look for a job in the town

Well, the girl ran off with someone else, the tariffs took all my pay
And here I stand where the old home stood before they took it away

Now the geese fly South & the cold wind moans as I stand here & hang my head
I've lost my love, I've lost my home and now I wish I was dead
Chorus

The Dillards / There Is a Time
JD Crow & The New South / The New South

94

Old Joe Clark

Traditional

Up Tempo

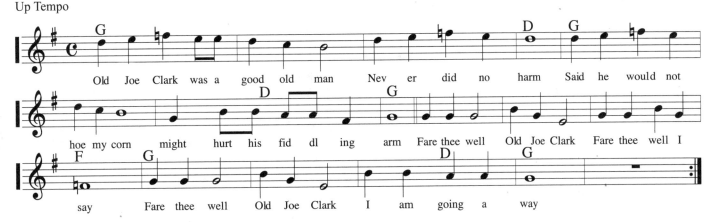

Old Joe Clark was a good old man Nev er did no harm Said he would not
hoe my corn might hurt his fid dl ing arm Fare thee well Old Joe Clark Fare thee well I
say Fare thee well Old Joe Clark I am going a way

G
Old Joe Clark was a good old man
D
Never did no harm
G.
Said he would not hoe my corn
D   **G**
Might hurt his fiddling arm

G
Fare thee well Old Joe Clark
F
Fare thee well I say
G
Fare thee well Old Joe Clark
D   **G**
I am going away

Chorus

I went down to Old Joe's house
Never been there before
He slept on a feather bed
And I slept on the floor
Chorus

I went down to Old Joe's house
Old Joe wasn't home
Ate up all of Old Joe's meat
And left Old Joe the bone
Chorus

I went down to Old Joe's house
He invited me to supper
Stumped my toe on a table leg
And stuck my nose in the butter
Chorus

The Dillards / Homecoming And Family Reunion
Goose Island Ramblers / Best of the Goose Island Ramblers
Doc and Merle Watson / Home Sweet Home

Old Train

Herb & Nikki Pedersen

Old train, I can hear your whistle blow
And I won't be jumping on again
Old train, I've been everywhere you go
And I know what lies beyond each bend

Chorus

Old train, each time you pass you're older than the last
And it seems I'm too old for running
I hear your rusted wheels grate against the rails
They cry with every mile
And I think I'll stay a while

Old train, I grow weary at the miles
And I miss the freedom that was mine
Old train, just to think about those times
I'll smile when you're high balling by
Chorus

Tony Rice Unit / Manzanita
Seldom Scene / Old Train
John Denver / All Aboard!

© 1974 Dear Friends Music (ASCAP)
All Rights Reserved. Used by Permission

Ole Slewfoot

Hausey & Webb

Up Tempo

High on a mountain, tell me what do you see
Bear tracks, bear tracks, coming after me
Better get your rifle, boy, before it's too late
That bear's got a little pig and headed for the gate

He's big around the middle and he's broad across the rump
Making ninety miles an hour taking thirty feet a jump
Ain't never been caught, he ain't never been treed
Some folks say he looks a lot like me

I saved up my money and I bought me some bees
And started making honey way up in the trees
Cut down the trees, but the honey's all gone
Old Slewfoot done made himself a home
Chorus

Winter's coming on and it's forty below
The river's froze over so where can he go
We'll chase him up the gully, then we'll chase him in the well
And we'll kick him in the bottom just to listen to him yell
Chorus

Chorus

One Way Track

Skaggs & Golding

Up Tempo

Well, she left me this morning
I heard her hanging on
Won't you hear that whistle blow
I don't know what I done
Must of had too much fun
And Lord I hate to see her go

Chorus

My heart's breaking, Lord it's taking
Me on a one way trip on down the track
My soul is burning, wheels are turning
Hey, Mister Engineer won't you bring my baby back

I'm on a one way track, one way don't come back
Just keep a going on and on
It's down in my soul, I'm about to lose control
And there's just one thing you must know
Chorus

Pallet On Your Floor

Traditional

Up Tempo

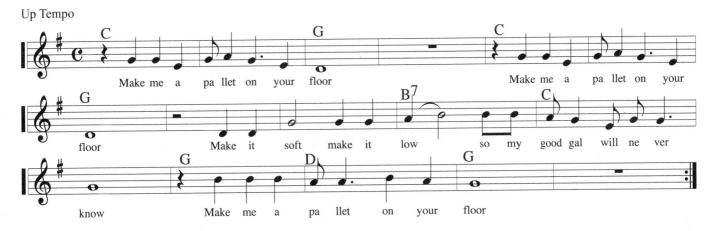

Chorus

  C   G
Make me a pallet on your floor
  C   G
Make me a pallet on your floor
                 B7   C
Make it soft, make it low so my good gal will never know
 G   D   G
Make me a pallet on your floor

These blues are everywhere I see
Weary blues arc everywhere I see
Blues all around me, everywhere I see
Nobody's had these blues like me
Chorus

Come all you good time friends of mine
Come all you good time friends of mine
When I had a dollar you treated me just fine
Where'd you go when I only had a dime
Chorus

I'd be more than satisfied
If I could catch a train and ride
When I reach Atlanta and have no place to go
Won't you make me a pallet on your floor
Chorus

Panama Red

Peter Rowan

Chorus

Panama Red, Panama Red
He'll steal your woman, then he'll steal your head
Panama Red, Panama Red
On his white horse, Mescalito, he comes breezing through town
I bet your woman's up in bed with old Panama Red

The judge don't know when Red's in town
He keeps well hidden underground
But everybody's acting lazy falling out and hanging round
My woman said, "Hey Pedro, you're acting crazy like a clown"
Nobody feels like working, Panama Red is back in town
Chorus

Everybody's looking out for him cause they know Red's satisfied
Little girls up and listen to him sing and tell sweet lies
Whenever things get too confusing, honey, we're better off in bed
And I'm searching all the joints in town for Panama Red
Chorus

New Riders of the Purple Sage / Adventures of Panama Red
Old & In The Way / Old & In The Way
Rollin' In The Hay / Live At The Oasis

100

Pig In A Pen

Traditional

Up Tempo

I got a pig at home in a pen corn to feed him on
all I need is a pretty young girl to feed him when I'm gone

Chorus

I got a pig at home in a pen *(G)*
Corn to feed him on *(C)*
All I need's a pretty little girl *(G)*
To feed him when I'm gone *(D)(G)*

Going up on a mountain
To sow a little cane
Raise a barrel of sorghum
Sweet little Liza Jane
Chorus

Black smoke a rising
Sure sign of rain
Put that old gray bonnet
On little Liza Jane
Chorus

Yonder comes that gal of mine
How do you think I know
Tell by that gingham gown
Hanging down so low
Chorus

Bake them biscuits, baby
Bake 'em good and brown
When you get them biscuits baked
We're Alabama bound
Chorus

Poor Wayfaring Stranger

Traditional

Slow Tempo

I'm just a poor way far ing stran ger Travel ing through this world of
woe But there's no sick ness toil or dan ger in that bright world to which I
go I'm go ing there to meet my Fa ther I'm go ing there no more to
roam I'm just a go ing o ver Jor dan I'm just a go ing o ver home

Chorus

I'm just a poor wayfaring stranger *(Em)*
Traveling through this world of woe *(Am)* *(B7)*
But there's no sickness toil or danger *(Em)*
In that bright world to which I go *(Am)* *(Em)*

I'm going there to meet my Father *(C)* *(G)*
I'm going there no more to roam *(C)* *(B7)*
I'm just a going over Jordan *(Em)*
I'm just a going over home *(Am)* *(Em)*

I'll soon be free from every trial
My body asleep in the old graveyard
I'll drop the cross of self denial
And enter on my great reward
Chorus

Joan Baez / David's Album
Emmylou Harris / Roses In The Snow
Tony Rice / Cold on the Shoulder
Doc & Merle Watson / Remembering Merle

102

Precious Memories

Traditional

Slow

Precious mem ories un seen an gels sent from some where to my soul

how they lin ger e ver near me and the sa cred past un fold

Pre cious mem ories how they lin ger how they e ver flood my soul

in the still ness of the midnight pre cious sa cred scenes un fold

    G   **C**   **G**
Precious memories, unseen angels
                  D
Sent from somewhere to my soul
G   **C**   **G**
How they linger ever near me
    D   **G**
And the sacred past unfold

Chorus

    G
Precious memories, how they linger
C   **G**
How they ever flood my soul
          C   **G**
In the stillness of the midnight
     D   **G**
Precious sacred scenes unfold

Precious father, loving mother
Fly across the lonely years
And old home scenes of my childhood
In fond memory appear

As I travel on life's pathway
Know not what the years may hold
As I ponder, hope grows fonder
Precious memories flood my soul

In the still of the midnight
Echoes from the past I hear
Old time singing, gladness bringing
From that lovely land somewhere

Pretty Polly

Traditional

Up Tempo

Oh Polly pretty Polly come go a long with me Polly pretty Polly come go a long with me Before we get married some pleasures to see

Oh Polly, pretty Polly, come go along with me
Polly, pretty Polly, come go along with me
Before we get married some pleasures to see

He rode her oer hills and valleys so deep
He rode her oer hills and valleys so deep
Pretty Polly mistrusted and then began to weep

Oh Willie, oh Willie, I'm afraid of your ways
Oh Willie, oh Willie, I'm afraid of your ways
The way you've been acting, you'll lead me astray

Oh Polly, pretty Polly, your guess is bout right
Oh Polly, pretty Polly, your guess is out right
I dug on your grave the best part of last night

She knelt down before him pleading for her life
She knelt down before him pleading for her life
Please let me be a single girl if I can't be your wife

He stabbed her in the heart and her heart's blood did flow
He stabbed her in the heart and her heart's blood did flow
And into the grave pretty Polly did go

He went down to the jailhouse and what did he say
He went down to the jailhouse and what did he say
I killed pretty Polly and tried to get away

Oh gentleman and ladies, I bid you farewell
Oh gentleman and ladies, I bid you farewell
For killing pretty Polly my soul will go to hell

Ralph Stanley / Bound To Ride
Wilma Lee Cooper / Classic Country Favorites
David Grisman / Home Is Where The Heart Is

Rain And Snow

Traditional

Medium Tempo

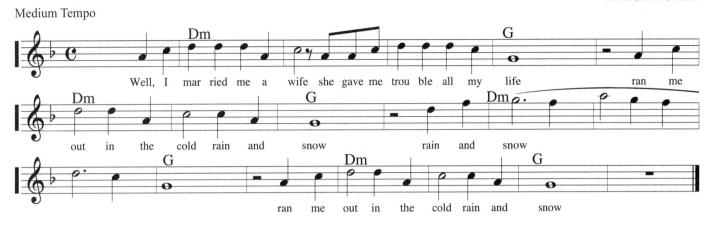

Well, I married me a wife ^{Dm}
She gave me trouble all my life ^G
Ran me ^{Dm}out in the cold rain and ^Gsnow
Rain and snow ^{Dm}^G
Ran me ^{Dm}out in the cold rain and ^Gsnow

Well, she came down this path
Combing back her long yellow hair
And her cheeks were as red as the rose
As the rose
And her cheeks were as red as the rose

Well, I did all I could do
To try to get along with you
And I'm not a gonna be treated this a way
This a way
And I'm not a gonna be treated this a way

Well, she came in my room
Where she met a painful doom
And I'm not gonna be treated this a way
This a way
And I'm not a gonna be treated this a way

Rank Stranger To Me

Albert Brumley

Medium Waltz

I wandered again to my home in the mountains (G, D, G)
Where in youth's early dawn I was happy and free (D)
I looked for my friends, but I never could find them (G, D, G)
I found they were all rank strangers to me (D, G, C, G)

Chorus

Everybody I met seemed to be a rank stranger
No Mother or Dad, not a friend could I see (D)
They knew not my name and I knew not their faces (G, D, G)
I found they were all rank strangers to me (D, G)

They've all moved away, said the voice of a stranger
To a beautiful home by the bright crystal sea
Some beautiful day, I'll meet them in heaven
Where no one will be a stranger to me

Reuben's Train

Traditional

Medium Tempo

Reu ben had a train he put it on the track You could hear the whis tle

blow a hun dred miles Oh me Oh

my you can hear the whis tle blow a hun dred miles

D
Reuben had a train, he put it on the track
A   **D**
You could hear the whistle blow a hundred miles

Oh me, oh my
                              A   **D**
You can hear the whistle blow a hundred miles

I'm going to the East, I'm going to the West
I'm going where them chilly winds don't blow
Chorus

Oh, you ought to been uptown and seen that train come down
You could hear the whistle blow a hundred miles
Chorus

I'm walking these old ties with tears in my eyes
I'm trying to read a letter from my home
If that train runs right, I'll be home tomorrow night
Arriving on that Train 45
Chorus

Chorus (vertical text in left margin of chorus section)

Doc and Merle Watson / Home Sweet Home
Josh Graves / Josh Graves - King Of The Dobro
Tony Rice / Guitar

Rider

Auldridge, Duffey, Eldridge, Gray, Starling

Up Tempo

I know you rider gonna miss me when I'm gone
I know you rider gonna miss me when I'm gone
Gonna miss your baby from rolling in your arms

I lay down last night, Lord, could not take my rest
I lay down last night, Lord, could not take my rest
My mind was wandering like the wild geese in the West

The sun is gonna shine in my back door some day
The sun is gonna shine in my back door some day
The cold March wind's gonna blow my cares away

I wish I was a headlight on an East bound train
I wish I was a headlight on an East bound train
I'd shine my light through the cool Colorado rain

I know you rider gonna miss me when I'm gone
I know you rider gonna miss me when I'm gone
Gonna miss your baby from rolling in your arms

Seldom Scene / Act 3
Slack Family / Slack Family Bluegrass Band

108

Rocky Top

Bryant & Bryant

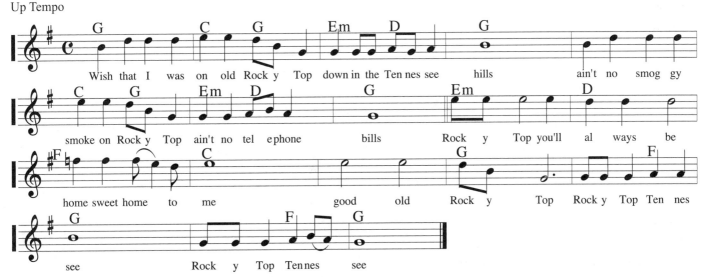

Up Tempo

Wish that I was on old Rock y Top down in the Ten nes see hills ain't no smog gy

smoke on Rock y Top ain't no tel e phone bills Rock y Top you'll al ways be

home sweet home to me good old Rock y Top Rock y Top Ten nes

see Rock y Top Ten nes see

G **C** **G**
Wish that I was on old Rocky Top
Em **D** **G**
Down in the Tennessee hills
C **G**
Ain't no smoggy smoke on Rocky Top
Em **D** **G**
Ain't no telephone bills

Once I had a girl on Rocky Top half bear the other half cat
Wild as a mink, but sweet as soda pop, I still dream about that

Chorus

Em **D**
Rocky Top, you'll always be
F **C**
Home, sweet home to me
G
Good old Rocky Top
F **G**
Rocky Top, Tennessee
F **G**
Rocky Top, Tennessee

Once two strangers climbed on Rocky Top looking for a moonshine still
Strangers ain't come down from Rocky Top, reckon they never will

Corn don't grow at all on Rocky Top, dirt's too rocky by far
That's why all the folks on Rocky Top get their corn from a jar
Chorus

I've had years of cramped up city life trapped like a duck in a pen
All I know is it's a pity life can't be simple again
Chorus

The Osborne Brothers / Rocky Top '96
The Bluegrass Band / Once Again From The Top
Jim & Jesse / The Old Dominion Masters

109

Roll In My Sweet Baby's Arms

Traditional

Up Tempo

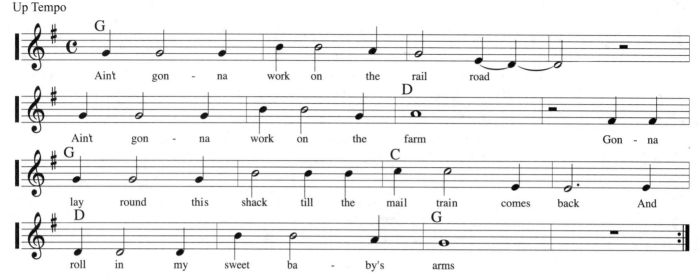

Ain't gon - na work on the rail road
Ain't gon - na work on the farm Gon - na
lay round this shack till the mail train comes back And
roll in my sweet ba - by's arms

G
Ain't gonna work on the railroad
Ain't gonna work on the farm **D**
Gonna lay around this shack till the **C** mail train comes back
And **D** roll in my sweet baby's **G** arms

Chorus

Roll in my sweet baby's arms
Roll in my sweet baby's arms
Gonna lay around this shack till the mail train comes back
And roll in my sweet baby's arms

Where were you last Saturday night
While I was laying down in jail
You were out walking the street with another man
Wouldn't even try to go my bail

Mama was a beauty operator
Sister could weave and spin
Daddy's got an interest in an old cotton mill
Watch that money roll in

I know your parents don't like me
They run me away from your door
If I had my life to live over again
I wouldn't go back there no more

Roll Muddy River

Betty Perry

Chorus

Roll, muddy river, roll on muddy river roll on
I've got a notion you'll go to the ocean alone
Cause I've got a baby in Tennessee
Who's long been a-waiting for little old me
So roll muddy river, roll on muddy river roll on

Three long months on a sand barge tour
How much more can a man endure
It's high time I was home for sure
So roll, muddy river, roll on
Chorus

New Orleans on to old St. Lou, stopped by Memphis, Minneapolis, too
Back in Nashville I'll be through, so roll, muddy river, roll on
Chorus

I love you but just call it fate, you and I are gonna separate
You'll be here but she won't wait, so roll, muddy river, roll on
Chorus

111

Roll On Buddy

Traditional

Up Tempo

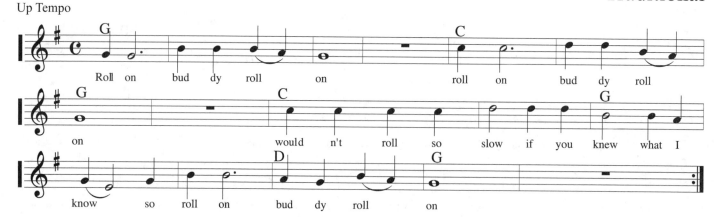

Chorus

> G
> Roll on buddy, roll on
> C   G
> Roll on buddy, roll on
> C   G
> Wouldn't roll so slow if you knew what I know
> D   G
> So roll on buddy, roll on

I'm going to that east pay road
I'm going to that east pay road
I'm going to the East, I'm going to the West
I'm going to the one I love best

My home is down in Tennessee
My home is down in Tennessee
In sunny Tennessee, that's where I want to be
Way down in sunny Tennessee

I've got a good woman just the same
I've got a good woman just the same
I've got a good woman and I'm gonna change her name
I've got a good woman just the same

Bill Monroe / The Music of Bill Monroe: 1958 - 1969

Roses In The Snow

Ruth Franks

I met my darling in the springtime
When all the flowers were in bloom
And like the flowers our love blossomed
We married in the month of June

Our love was like a burning ember
It warmed us as a golden glow
We had sunshine in December
And threw our roses in the snow

Now God has taken my darling
And left me with a memory
A memory I will always cherish
Are these last words he said to me
Chorus

My darling's buried on the hillside
Where all the wild spring flowers grow
And when winter snows start falling
On his grave I'll place a rose
Chorus

Chorus (printed vertically, left of stanza 2)

113

Emmylou Harris / Roses In The Snow

Roving Gambler

Traditional

Up Tempo

I am a rov ing gam bler gam bled all a round When e ver I meet with a
deck of cards I lay my mon ey down lay my mon ey down lay my mon ey down

I am a roving gambler, gambled all around
Whenever I meet with a deck of cards I lay my money down
Lay my money down, lay my money down

I had not been in Frisco many more weeks than three
I met up with a pretty little girl, she fell in love with me
Fell in love with me, fell in love with me

She took me in her parlor, she cooled me with her fan
Whispered low in her Mother's ear, I love this gambling man
Love this gambling man, love this gambling man

Oh daughter, oh dear daughter, how can you treat me so
Leave your dear old mother and with the gambler go
With the gambler go, with the gambler go

Oh mother, oh dear mother, I'll tell you if I can
If you ever see me coming back, I'll be with a gambling man
With the gambling man, with the gambling man

I left her in Frisco, I wound up in Maine
I met up with a gambling man, we got in a poker game
Got in a poker game, got in a poker game

He put his money in the pot and dealt the cards around
Saw him deal from the bottom of the deck so I shot him down
Shot the gambler down, shot the gambler down

Now I'm down in prison, got a number for my name
Warden said as he locked the door, you've gambled your last game
Gambled you last game, gambled your last game

114

Salty Dog Blues

Traditional

Up Tempo

Standing on the cor ner with the low down blues great big hole in the bot tom of my shoes ho ney let me be your Sal ty Dog Let me be your Sal ty Dog or I won't be your man at all ho ney let me be your Sal ty Dog

Chorus

$\overset{\text{G}}{\text{S}}$tanding on the corner with the $\overset{\text{E}}{\text{low}}$ down blues
$\overset{\text{A}7}{\text{Gr}}$eat big hole in the bottom of my shoes
$\overset{\text{D}}{\text{H}}$oney, let me be your salty d$\overset{\text{G}}{\text{o}}$g

Let me be your $\overset{\text{E}}{\text{s}}$alty dog
Or I $\overset{\text{A}7}{\text{won}}$'t be your man at all$\overset{\text{G}}{}$
$\overset{\text{D}}{\text{H}}$oney let me be your salty d$\overset{\text{G}}{\text{o}}$g

Now look a hear Sal, I know you
Run down stocking and worn out shoes
Honey let me be your salty dog
Chorus

I was down in the wildwood setting on a log
Finger on the trigger and an eye on the hog
Honey let me be your salty dog
Chorus

I pulled the trigger and the gun said go
Shot fell over in Mexico
Honey let me be your salty dog
Chorus

Satan's Jewel Crown

Clifford Waldron

Slow Waltz

Now if I were a Queen and a ruler of nations
With diamonds and jewels profound
Well, I'd rather know that I had salvation
Than to know my reward would be Satan's jewel crown

Chorus

Satan's jewel crown I've worn it so long
But God for my soul has reached down
His love set me free, He made me his own
And helped me cast off Satan's jewel crown

Oh, the life that I live so sinful and needless
Drinking and running around
All the things that I do for the love of the devil
I know my reward will be Satan's jewel crown
Chorus

Emmylou Harris / Elite Hotel
Seldom Scene / 25th Anniversary Celebration

Shady Grove

Traditional

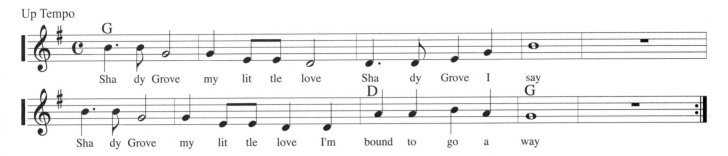

Shady Grove my little love
Shady Grove I say
Shady Grove my little love
I'm bound to go away

Cheeks as red as a blooming rose, eyes are the prettiest brown
She's the darling of my heart, sweetest girl in town
Chorus

I wish I had a big fine horse, corn to feed him on
And Shady Grove to stay at home and feed him when I'm gone
Chorus

Went to see my Shady Grove, she was standing in the door
Her shoes and stockings in her hand, her little bare feet on the floor
Chorus

When I was a little boy, I wanted a barlow knife
Now I want little Shady Grove to say she'll be my wife
Chorus

A kiss from pretty little Shady Grove is sweet as brandy wine
There ain't no girl in this old world that's prettier than mine
Chorus

Jerry Garcia & David Grisman / Shady Grove
Chesapeake / Rising Tide

Silver Dagger

Traditional

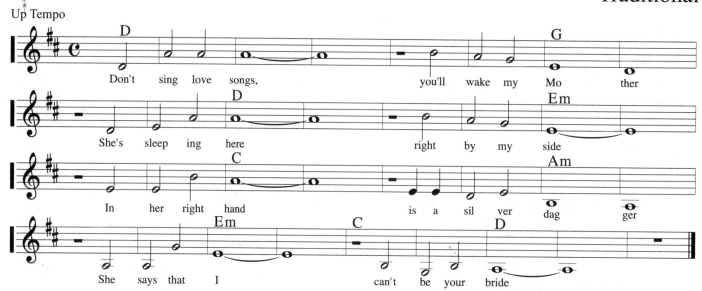

Up Tempo

D / Don't sing love songs, / you'll wake my Mo ther / G

She's sleep ing here / right by my side / D / Em

In her right hand / C / is a sil ver dag ger / Am

She says that I / Em / can't / C / be your bride / D

D Don't sing love songs, you'll wake my Mo**G**ther
She's sleeping here right by my **D**side **Em**
In her right hand is a silver dag**C**ger **Am**
She says that I can't be your **Em** **C** bride **D**

All men are fools so says my Mother
They'll tell you again loving lies
And then they'll go and court some other
Leaving you alone to cry inside

My Daddy is a handsome devil
He's got a chain five miles long
On every link a heart does dangle
Of another maid he's loved and wronged

Go court another tender maiden
In hopes that she might be your wife
For I've been warned so I've decided
I'll sleep alone all of my life

Singing All Day And Dinner On The Ground

Martin & Yates

Medium Tempo

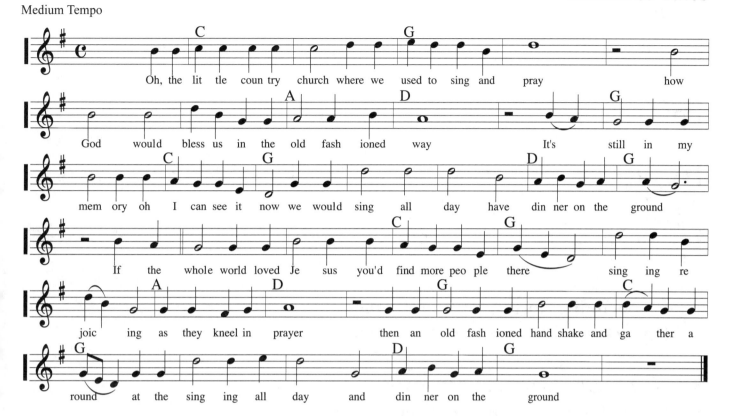

Oh, the lit tle coun try church where we used to sing and pray how God would bless us in the old fash ioned way It's still in my mem ory oh I can see it now we would sing all day have din ner on the ground If the whole world loved Je sus you'd find more peo ple there sing ing re joic ing as they kneel in prayer then an old fash ioned hand shake and ga ther a round at the sing ing all day and din ner on the ground

Chorus

Oh, the little church where we used to sing and pray
    C   G
How God would bless us in the old-fashioned way
                                  A   D
It's still in my memory, oh I can see it now
G   C   G
We would sing all day, have dinner on the ground
                        D   G

If the whole world loved Jesus you'd find more people there
                                            C   G
Singing, rejoicing as they kneel in prayer
              A   D
Then an old-fashioned handshake and gather around
        G   C   G
At the singing all day and dinner on the ground
                        D   G
Chorus

We would sing those old songs and the preacher would preach
Of how Jesus died for you and for me
You could feel the Great Spirit from Heaven pouring down
At the singing all day and dinner on the ground
Chorus

119

Jimmy Martin / Singing All Day & Dinner On The Ground

Sitting On Top Of The World

Traditional

Up Tempo

It was in the Spring one sun-ny day my good girl left me Lord she went a way now she's gone and I don't wor ry cause I'm sit-ting on top of the world

^GIt was in the Spring, one sunny day
^{G7}My good gal left me, Lord she went a^Cway ^G

Chorus

Now she's gone and I don't wo^{Em}rry
Cause I'm^G sitting on to^Dp of the ^Gworld^G

She called me up from El Paso
Said, "Come back, Daddy, Lord I need you so".
Chorus

Ashes to ashes, dust to dust
Show me a woman a man can trust
Chorus

Mississippi River long, deep, and wide
The woman I'm loving is on the other side
Chorus

You don't like my peaches, don't you shake my tree
Get out of my orchard, let my peaches be
Chorus

Don't you come here running, poking out your hand
I'll get me a woman like you got your man
Chorus

Bill Monroe / Blue Grass Style
Doc Watson / Vanguard
Seldom Scene / 15 Year Anniversary

120

Some Day

Tim Stafford

Medium Tempo

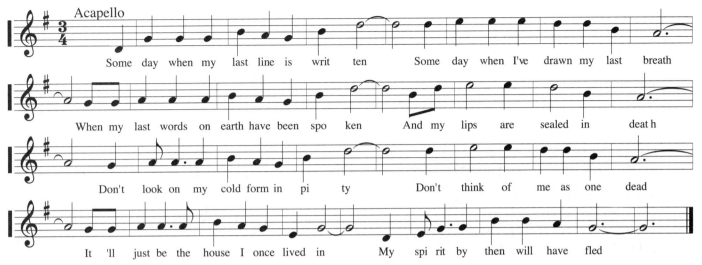

Some day when my last line is written
Some day when I've drawn my last breath
When my last words on earth have been spoken
And my lips are sealed in death
Don't look on my cold form in pity
Don't think of me as one dead
It'll just be the house I once lived in
My spirit by then will have fled

I'll have finished my time here allotted
But I won't be in darkness alone
I will have heard from heaven
The summons to come on home
And when my body is in the grave
Don't think that I'll be there
I won't be dead, but living
In the place Jesus went to prepare

And after all is said and done
Know that my last earnest prayer
Is that my love ones be ready
Some day to meet me there

Blue Highway / Midnight Storm

Sweet Sunny South

Traditional

Medium Tempo

Take me back to the place where I first saw the light
To the sweet sunny south, take me home
Where the mocking birds sang me to sleep in the night
Oh, why was I tempted to roam?

Take me back to the place where I first saw the light
To the sweet sunny south, take me home
Where the mockingbirds sang me to sleep in the night
Oh, why was I tempted to roam?

I think with regret of the dear home I left
Of the warm hearts that sheltered me there
Of wife and of dear ones of whom I'm bereft
For the old place again do I sigh

Take me back to the place where the orange trees grow
To my plot in the evergreen shade
Where the flowers from the river's green margin did grow
And spread their sweet scent through the glade

The path to our cottage they say has grown green
 And the place is quite lonely around
Where the flowers from the river's green margin did grow
And spread their sweet scent through the glade

But yet I'll return to the place of my birth
For the children have played round the door
Where they gathered wild blossoms that grew round the path
They will echo our footsteps no more

Take me back, let me see what is left that I knew
Can it be that the old house is gone?
Dear friends of my childhood indeed must be few
And I must face death all alone

The Bluegrass Album Band / Volume V
The Osborne Brothers / When The Roses Bloom In Dixieland
Garcia, Jerry & David Grisman / Shady Grove

122

Swing Low Sweet Chariot

Traditional

Medium Tempo

Chorus

I looked over Jordan and what did I see
Coming for to carry me home
A band of angels coming after me
Coming for to carry me home

Swing low sweet chariot
Coming for to carry me home
Swing low sweet chariot
Coming for to carry me home

If you get there before I do
Coming for to carry me home
Tell all my friends I'm coming, too
Coming for to carry me home
Chorus

I'm sometimes up and sometimes down
Coming for to carry me home
But still my soul feels heavenward bound
Coming for to carry me home
Chorus

Bill Monroe / Blue Grass Volume 2
Jim & Jesse / Old Country Church
Seldom Scene / Baptizing

Take Me In Your Lifeboat

Adcock & Duffey

Up Tempo

Chorus

G   C   G
Take me in your lifeboat, take me in your lifeboat
                              D
It will stand the raging storm
G   C   G
Take me in your lifeboat, take me in your lifeboat
                  D G
It will bear the spirit home

G   C   G
Come and brothers and sisters and don't fall asleep
                                          D
Pray night and day or you'll sleep in the deep
                          G   G
Now Fathers and Mothers are praying so loud
                          D   G
Oh, Lord won't you take us in your lifeboat
Chorus

Clouds are so heavy the wind is so loud
Thunder is rolling beckoning the crowd
They pray for their shipmates for what they have done
They took the dying sailor in their lifeboat
Chorus

Flatt & Scruggs / Flatt & Scruggs 1959 - 1963
Chris Hillman / Slippin' Away
Seldom Scene / 15th Anniversary Celebration,

Talk About Suffering

Traditional

Medium Tempo
Acapella

Talk about suffering here below and let's keep a loving Jesus
Talk about suffering here below and let's keep a following Jesus
The gospel train is coming, now don't you want to go
And leave this world of sorrow and troubles here below
Oh, can't you hear it Father and don't you want to go
And leave this world of sorrow and troubles here below

Talk about suffering here below and let's keep a loving Jesus
Talk about suffering here below and let's keep a following Jesus
Oh, can't you hear it Mother and don't you want to go
And leave this world of sorrow and troubles here below

Talk about suffering here below and let's keep a loving Jesus
Talk about suffering here below and let's keep a following Jesus
Oh, can't you hear it Brother and don't you want to go
And leave this world of sorrow and troubles here below
The gospel train is coming, now don't you want to go
And leave this world of sorrow and troubles here below

Ricky Skaggs & Tony Rice / Skaggs & Rice
Doc Watson / Doc Watson

125

Tennessee Stud

Jimmy Driftwood

Medium Tempo

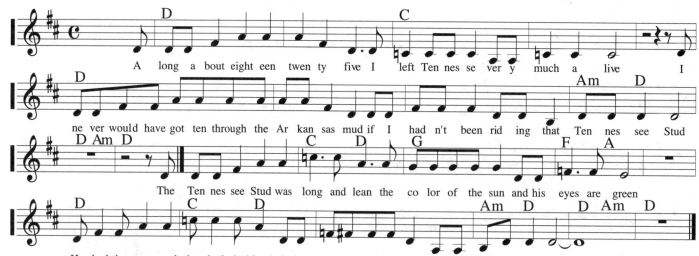

Chorus

Along about 1825 I left Tennessee very much alive
I never would have gotten through the Arkansas mud if I hadn't been riding that Tenn. Stud

I had some trouble with my sweet heart's Pa & one of her brothers was a bad outlaw
I sent her a letter by my Uncle Fudd & I road away on the Tennessee Stud

The Tennessee Stud was long and lean, the color of the sun and his eyes are green
He had the nerve and he had the blood & there never was a horse like the Tennessee Stud

We drifted on down to no man's land & crossed that river called the Rio Grande
I raced my horse with a Spaniard's foal till I got me a skin full of silver and gold

Me and the gambler, we couldn't agree, we got in a fight over Tennessee
We jerked our guns and he fell with a thud & I got away on the Tennessee Stud
Chorus

I got just as lonesome as a man could be, dreaming of my girl in Tennessee
The Tennessee Stud's green eyes turned blue cause he was dreaming of a sweetheart, too

We loped right back across Arkansas, I whooped her brothers and I whooped her Pa
I found that girl with the golden hair & the Tennessee Stud found the Tennessee mare
Chorus

Stirrup to stirrup and side to side, we crossed them mountains and the valley wide
We came to Big Muddy then we forded a flood on the Tennessee mare and the Tennessee Stud

There's a pretty little baby on the cabin floor & a little horse colt playing round the door
I love that girl with the golden hair & the Tennessee Stud loves the Tennessee mare
Chorus

There's More Pretty Girls Than One

Traditional

Medium Tempo

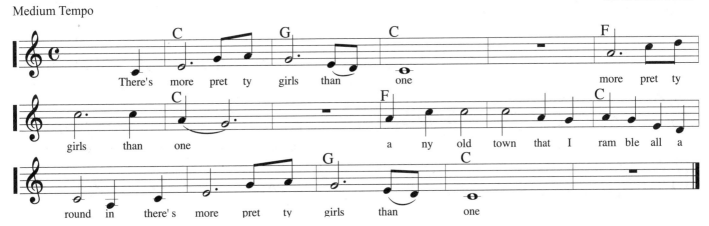

Chorus

There's more pretty girls than one
More pretty girls than one
Any old town that I ramble all around in
There's more pretty girls than one

Mama talked to me last night
She gave to me some good advice
She said, "Son, you oughta quit this old rambling around
And marry you a sweet loving wife".
Chorus

Honey, look down that old lonesome road
Hang down your pretty head and cry
Cause I'm thinking all about them pretty little gals
And hoping that I'll never die
Chorus

Ricky Skaggs & Tony Rice / Skaggs & Rice
Jimmy Martin / Jimmy Martin - 1954 - 1974
Arthel "Doc" Watson / The Vanguard Years

Think Of What You've Done

Tami LaRue

Up Tempo

Chorus

Is it true that I've lost you
Am I not the only one
After all this pain and sorrow
Darling, think of what you've done

Heart to heart, dear how I need you
Like the flowers need the dew
Loving you has been my life, dear
Can't believe we're really through
Chorus

I'll go back to old Virginia
Where the mountains meet the sky
In those hills I learned to love you
Let me stay there till I die
Chorus

Dan Fogelberg / High Country Snows
Ricky Skaggs / Bluegrass Rules
Hot Rize / Take It Home
Stanley Brothers / Stanley Brothers And Clinch Mountain Boys

This World Is Not My Home

Traditional

Medium Tempo

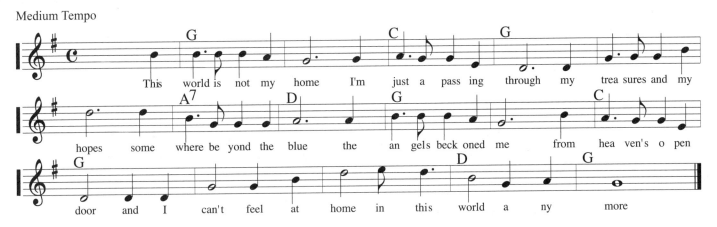

This world is not my home I'm just a passing through my treasures and my
hopes somewhere beyond the blue the angels beckoned me from heaven's open
door and I can't feel at home in this world anymore

This world is not my home I'm just a passing through
My treasures and my hopes somewhere beyond the blue
The angels beckoned me from heaven's open door
And I can't feel at home in this world anymore

Oh, Lord you know I have no friend like you
If heaven's not my home, then Lord what would I do?
The angel's beckoned me from heaven's open door
And I can't feel at home in this world anymore

I have a loving Mother over in Gloryland
I don't expect to stop until I shake her hand
She's waiting there for me in heaven's open door
And I can't feel at home in this world anymore
Chorus

Just o'er in Gloryland there'll be no dying there
The Saints will shout in victory and singing everywhere
I hear the voice of them that's gone on before
And I can't feel at home in this world anymore
Chorus

Jimmy Martin / Jimmy Martin, 1954 - 1974, Vol. 2
Flatt & Scruggs / 1948 -1959
Bill Monroe / Cryin' Holy Unto the Lord

Tom Dooley

Traditional

Chorus

G
Hang down your head Tom Dooley
Hang down your head and **D** cry
Hang down your head Tom Dooley
Poor boy you're bound to **G** die

I met her on the mountain
There I took her life
I met her on the mountain
Stabbed her with a knife
Chorus

Bout this time tomorrow
Reckon where I'll be
Hadn't of been for Grayson
I'd have been in Tennessee
Chorus

Bout this time tomorrow
Reckon where I'll be
Down in some lonesome canyon
Hanging from a white oak tree
Chorus

Kingston Trio - The Very Best of the Kingston Trio
Grateful Dead - Reckoning - Disc 2
Doc Watson - The Essential Doc Watson

Train, Train

Shorty Medlock

Up Tempo

C

Train, train, gonna take you on out of this
town Train, train, gon na
take you on out of this town Well, that man I'm in love with
Lord, he's Mem phis bound

C
Train, train, gonna take you on out of this town
Bb   C
Train, train, gonna take you on out of this town
Well, that man I'm in love with
G
Bb   F   C
Lord, he's Memphis bound

He's leaving here, like a raggedy old goat
He's leaving me, that no good so and so
That man I'm in love with
Lord, he wants to go

Goodbye, goodbye, I'll find myself another man
Goodbye, goodbye, I'll find myself another man
You take that night train to Memphis
Me, I'll make new plans
Take that night train to Memphis
Leave while you can

131

Troubles Up And Down The Road

Traditional

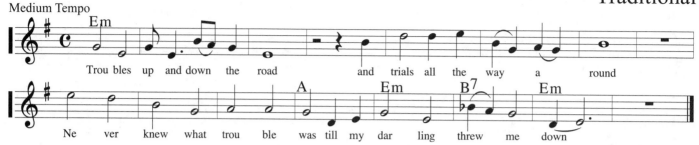

Em
Troubles up and down the road and trials all the way around
Never knew what trouble **A** was
Till **Em** my darling **B7** threw me **Em** down

If ever I meet that girl again our troubles will all be o'er
I'll steal her out away from home
We will sail for some foreign shore

When my worldly trials are over and my last goodbye I've said
Bury me near my darling's door
Where the roses bloom and fade

My pockets are all empty like they've often been before
If ever I reach my home again
I'll walk these ties no more

The cheapest thing I ever done was sleeping out among the pines
The hardest thing I ever tried
Was keeping your loving off my mind

I've never worked for pleasure, peace on earth I cannot find
The only thing I surely own
Is a worried and troubled mind

Troubles up and down the road and trial all the way around
Never knew what trouble was
Till my darling threw me down

132

Turn Your Radio On

Albert E. Brumley

Chorus

Come & listen in to a radio station where the mighty hosts of Heaven sing
Turn your radio on (echo), turn your radio on (echo)
If you wanna hear the songs of Zion coming from the land of endless spring
Get in touch with God (echo), turn your radio on (echo)

Turn your radio on (echo) and listen to the music in the air
Turn your radio on (echo), Heaven's glory share (echo)
Turn the lights down low (echo) and listen to the Master's radio
Get in touch with God (echo), turn your radio on (echo)

Brother, listen in to the Gloryland chorus, listen to the glad hosannas roll
Turn your radio on (echo), turn your radio on (echo)
Get a little taste of joy awaiting, get a little Heaven in your soul
Turn your radio on (echo), turn your radio on (echo)
Chorus

Listen to the songs of the Fathers & the Mothers & the many friends gone
on before
Turn your radio on (echo), turn your radio on (echo)
Some eternal morning we shall meet them over on the hallelujah shore
Turn your radio on (echo), turn your radio on (echo)
Chorus

John Hartford / Aero-plain
The Hee Haw Gospel Quartet / The Best Of The Hee Haw Gospel Quartet

133

Uncloudy Day

Traditional

Up Tempo

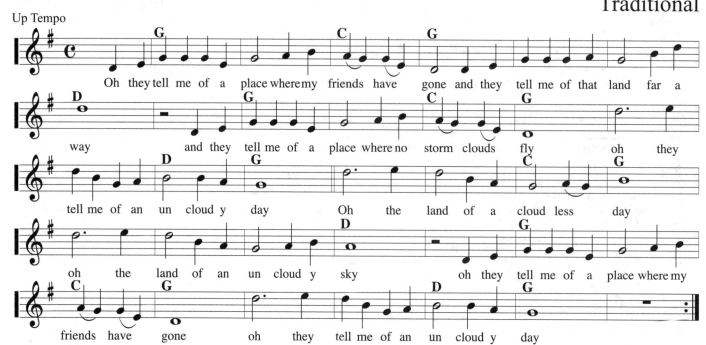

Oh, they tell me of a place where my friends have gone
$\overset{G}{}$ $\overset{C}{}$ $\overset{G}{}$
And they tell me of that land far away
$\overset{D}{}$
And they tell me of a place where no storm clouds fly
$\overset{G}{}$ $\overset{C}{}$ $\overset{G}{}$
Oh, they tell me of an uncloudy day
$\overset{D}{}$ $\overset{G}{}$

Chorus

Oh, the land of a cloudless day
Oh, the land of an uncloudy sky
They tell me of a place where my friends have gone
Oh, they tell me of an uncloudy day

Oh, they tell me that he smiles on his children's face
Oh, his smile drives their sorrow away
And they tell me that no tears ever come again
Oh, they tell me of an uncloudy day
Chorus

Oh, they tell me of a home far beyond the sky
And they tell me of a home far away
And they tell me of a home where no storm clouds fly
Oh, they tell me of an uncloudy day
Chorus

Willie Nelson / On The Road Again
Ralph Stanley / Songs My Mother Taught Me And More
Doc Watson / On Praying Ground

Wabash Cannonball

Traditional

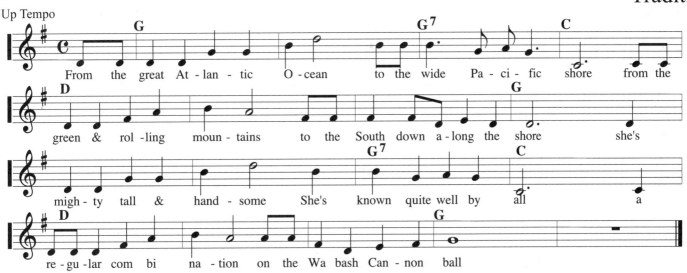

From the great Atlantic Ocean to the wide Pacific shore
From the green & rolling mountains to the South down along the shore
She's mighty tall and handsome, she's known quite well by all
A regular combination on the Wabash Cannonball

She came down from Birmingham one cold December day
As she rolled into the station, you could hear all the people say
There's a girl from Tennessee, she's long and she's tall
She came down from Birmingham on the Wabash Cannonball

Our Eastern states are dandy, so the people always say
From New York to St. Louis and Chicago by the way
From the hills of Minnesota where the rippling waters fall
No changes can be taken on the Wabash Cannonball

Here's to Daddy Claxton, may his name forever stand
And always be remembered round the courts of Alabam
His Earthly race is over and the curtains round him fall
We'll carry him home to victory on the Wabash Cannonball

Listen to the jingle, the rumble, and the roar
As she glides along the woodlands through the hills and by the shore
Hear the mighty rush of the engine, hear the lonesome hobo's call
As she rambles across the country on the Wabash Cannonball

Way Downtown

Traditional

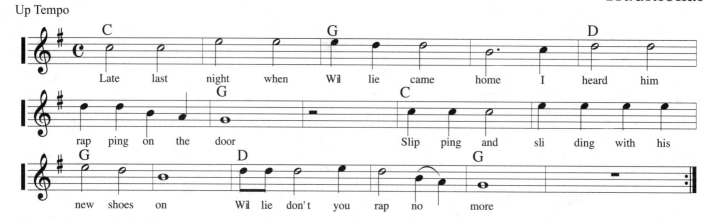

Late last night when Willie came home
I heard him rapping on the door
Slipping and sliding with his new shoes on
Willie don't you rap no more

Chorus

Oh, me, oh, my
What's gonna become of me
Way downtown fooling around
Mama don't you cry for me

One old shirt is all I've got
And a dollar is all I crave
Brought nothing with me into this world
Gonna take nothing to my grave
Chorus

Wish I was down in Old Baltimore
Sitting in an easy chair
One arm around my old guitar
And the other around my dear
Chorus

Wish I had a needle and thread
As fine as I could sew
Sew all the good looking girls to my back
And down the road I'd go
Chorus

Doc Watson / Will The Circle Be Unbroken
Tony Rice / Tony Rice

136

Were You There

Traditional

Slow Tempo

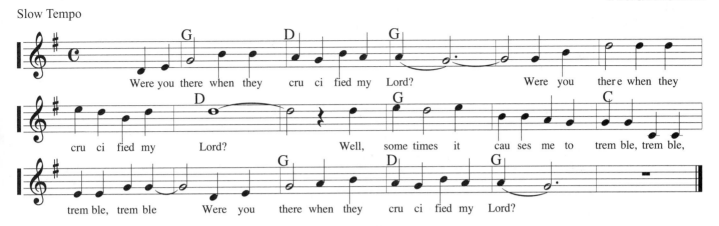

Were you there when they cru ci fied my Lord? Were you there when they
cru ci fied my Lord? Well, some times it cau ses me to trem ble, trem ble,
trem ble, trem ble Were you there when they cru ci fied my Lord?

Were you there when they crucified my Lord?
Were you there when they crucified my Lord?
Well, sometimes it causes me to tremble, tremble, tremble, tremble
Were you there when they crucified my Lord?

Were you there when they laid him in the tomb?
Were you there when they laid him in the tomb?
Were you there when they laid him in the tomb?
Well, sometimes it causes me to tremble, tremble, tremble, tremble
Were you there when they laid him in the tomb?

Were you there when they nailed him to the cross?
Were you there when they nailed him to the cross?
Were you there when they nailed him to the cross?
Well, sometimes it causes me to tremble, tremble, tremble, tremble
Were you there when they nailed him to the cross?

Were you there when they crucified my Lord?
Were you there when they crucified my Lord?
Well, sometimes it causes me to tremble, tremble, tremble, tremble
Were you there when they crucified my Lord?

Seldom Scene / Baptizing
Johnny Cash / The Man In Black (1959-1962)
Ricky Skaggs / Soldier Of The Cross

When The Golden Leaves Begin To Fall

Albert Price

Medium Waltz

I left the one I loved in the mountains
And all the love we shared
But each night as she kneels by her bedside
I know she calls my name in her prayers

Chorus

When the moon shines on the Blue Ridge Mountains
And it seems I can hear my sweetheart call
How I long to be near my darling
When the golden leaves begin to fall

She knows I'll return to the mountains
And will bring to her a wedding ring
I will place upon her finger
Happiness to both it will bring
Chorus

Wintertime is so cold in the mountains
The ground will soon be covered white with snow
How I long to keep the home fires burning
For I know my darling needs me so
Chorus

Bill Monroe / Blue Grass Volume 1
Peter Rowan / The First Whippoorwill

When The Roll Is Called Up Yonder

Traditional

Medium Tempo

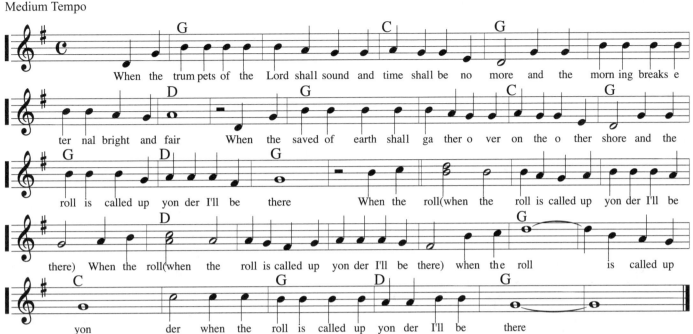

When the trum pets of the Lord shall sound and time shall be no more and the morn ing breaks e ter nal bright and fair When the saved of earth shall ga ther o ver on the o ther shore and the roll is called up yon der I'll be there When the roll(when the roll is called up yon der I'll be there) When the roll(when the roll is called up yon der I'll be there) when the roll is called up yon der when the roll is called up yon der I'll be there

When the $\overset{G}{\text{trumpet}}$ of the Lord shall sound and $\overset{C}{\text{time}}$ shall be no $\overset{G}{\text{more}}$
And the morning breaks eternal bright and $\overset{D}{\text{fair}}$
When the $\overset{G}{\text{saved}}$ of earth shall gather over $\overset{C}{\text{on}}$ the other $\overset{G}{\text{shore}}$
And the roll is called up $\overset{D}{\text{yonder}}$ I'll be $\overset{G}{\text{there}}$

Chorus

When the $\overset{G}{\text{roll}}$ (When the roll is called up yonder I'll be there)
When the $\overset{D}{\text{roll}}$ (When the roll is called up yonder I'll be there)
When the $\overset{G}{\text{roll}}$ is called up $\overset{C}{\text{yonder}}$ I'll be there
When the $\overset{G}{\text{roll}}$ is called up $\overset{D}{\text{yonder}}$ I'll be $\overset{G}{\text{there}}$

On that bright and cloudless morning when the dead in Christ shall rise
And the glory of His resurrection share
When His chosen ones shall gather to their home beyond the skies
And the roll is called up yonder I'll be there
Chorus

Let us labor for the Master from the dawn till setting sun
Let us talk of all His wondrous love and care
Then when all of life is over and our work on earth is done
And the roll is called up yonder I'll be there
Chorus

139

When The Saints Go Marching In

Traditional

Up Tempo

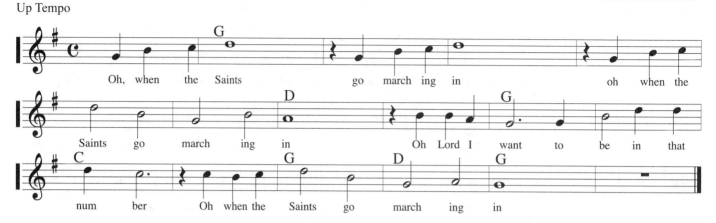

Oh, when the Saints go march ing in oh when the

Saints go march ing in Oh Lord I want to be in that

num ber Oh when the Saints go march ing in

Oh, when the **G** saints go marching in
Oh, when the saints go marching in **D**
Oh, Lord I **G** want to be in that **C** number
Oh, when the Saints **G** go **D** marching in **G**

And when they crown him King of Kings
And when they crown him King of Kings
Oh, Lord I want to be in that number
Oh, when they crown him King of Kings

And when they crown him Lord of Lords
And when they crown him Lord of Lords
Oh, Lord I want to be in that number
Oh, when they crown him Lord of Lords

And in that sweet by and by
And in that sweet by and by
Oh, Lord I want to be in that number
In that sweet by and by

Kingston Trio / American Troubadours
Louis Armstrong / When The Saints Go Marchin' In
Elvis Presley / The Million Dollar Quartet

140

When The Storm Is Over

Bob Lucas

Up Tempo

Chorus

G D   G   D   Em   D G
I will fly away when the storm is over
G D   G   D   Em   D G
I will fly away when the storm is over
C   G
And I'll be back in the Spring
         C   G
When the robins chirp and the red bird sings
G D   G   D   Em   D G Bm C Bm C G D G
I will fly away when the storm is over

   G   D   C   Bm
The chestnut mare is meek & mild
   C   G   G
You know she's Mother Nature's child
G   D   C   Bm
She stands undaunted in the rain
  C   D   G
The water drips off tail and mane

Ponies in the field dancing in the clover
Ponies are in the field dancing in the clover
I'll scratch your back if you'll scratch mine
And we'll have a real good, real good time
I will fly away when the storm is over
Chorus

141

New Grass Revival / When The Storm Is Over

When You Go Walking

Roy McMillan

Chorus

When you go walking after midnight (G)
Over on the wrong side of town (C)
Walk down any street, many lost souls you'll meet (G)
Who's lives are broken like mine (D) (G)

You'll find souls wandering out in darkness
Whose place in life they'll never find
Wandering so aimless and hopelessly
Who's lives are broken like mine
Chorus

Thank God, you've got a home to go to
And a woman's love to keep you warm
You won't find the stars in the honky tonks and bars
Go home to your woman's loving arms
Chorus

Lonesome River Band / One Step Forward

Where The Soul Never Dies

Traditional

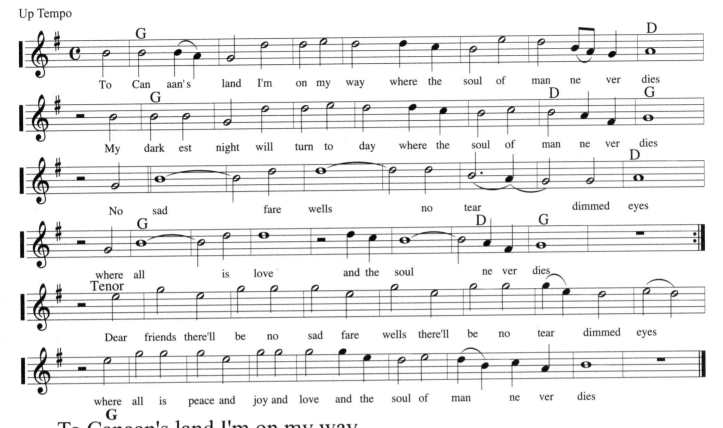

To Canaan's land I'm on my way
Where the soul (of man) never dies
My darkest night will turn to day
Where the soul (of man) never dies

No sad farewells, no tear dimmed eyes
Where all is love and the soul (of man) never dies

A rose is blooming there for me where the soul never dies
And I will spend eternity where the soul never dies   Chorus

A love-light beams across the foam where the soul never dies
It shines to light the shores of home where the soul never dies Chorus

My life will end in deathless sleep where the soul never dies
And everlasting joys I'll reap where the soul never dies   Chorus

I'm on my way to that fair land where the soul never dies
Where there will be no parting hand where the soul never dies Chorus

Ricky Skaggs & Tony Rice / Skaggs & Rice
Willie & Bobbie Nelson / I'd Rather Have Jesus
Hylo Brown / 20 Gospel Favorites

143

White House Blues

Traditional

Look here you rascal see what you've done you shot my hus band and

I've got you gun car ry me back to Wash ing ton

G
Look here you rascal, see what you've done
C   G
You shot my husband and I've got your gun
         D   G
Carry me back to Washington

McKinley hollered, McKinley squalled
Doctor said, "McKinley, I can't find the cause
You're bound to die, you're bound to die".

He jumped on his horse, he pulled on his mane
Said, "Listen you horse, you got to out run this train
From Buffalo to Washington".

The doctor come a running, took off his specs
Said, "Mr. McKinley, better cash in your checks
You're bound to die, you're bound to die".

Roosevelt's in the White House, doing his best
McKinley's in the graveyard, taking his rest
He's gone, he's gone

Bill Monroe and His Blue Grass Boys / Mule Skinner Blues
Doc Watson & Family / Treasures Untold
Muleskinner / A Potpourri Of Bluegrass Jam
IIIrd Tyme Out / Live At The MAC

144

Whither Thou Go

Tim Stafford

Medium Tempo

Acapello

Whi ther thou go (there I go), whi ther thou go (there I go) Whi ther thou go (there I go) Thy peo ple shall be my peo ple thy God my God (thy God my God) Ruth came down (wo man to Mo hab) Ruth came down (to the land of the He brew) Ruth came down (went on down) To the place that God an noint ed thy God my God (thy God my God)

Chorus

Whither thou go (there I go)
Whither thou go (there I go)
Whither thou go (there I go)
Thy people shall be my people thy God my God (thy God my God)

Ruth came down (woman to Mohab)
Ruth came down (to the land of the Hebrew)
Ruth came down (went on down)
To the place that God anointed thy God my God (thy God my God)
Chorus

Naomi came down (lost her husband)
Naomi came down (and her only son)
Naomi came down (she went on down)
To the land of milk and honey thy God my God (thy God my God)
Chorus

She said behold (your sister is gone)
She said behold (back to her God)
She said behold (come and go your way)
They lifted up their voices and wept again (they wept again)
Chorus

Blue Highway / Midnight Storm

Wildwood Flower

Traditional

Oh, ^GI'll twine with my ringlets and w^Daving black hai^{G.}r
With the roses so red and th^De lilies s^Go fair
And the myrtle so bright with the e^Cmerald hu^Ge
The pale aronatus with ey^Des of bright blu^Ge

I will dance, I will sing, and my life shall be gay
I will charm every heart and his crown I will sway
When I woke from my dream and my idols of clay
Our portion of love had all gone away

Oh, he taught me to love him and promise to love
Through ill and misfortune all others above
How my heart is now wondering no misery can tell
He's left me no warning, no word of farewell

Oh, he taught me to love him, he called me his flower
That was blooming to cheer him through life's dreary hour
Oh, I longed to see him and regret the dark hour
He's gone and neglected this pale wildwood flower

Will The Circle Be Unbroken

Traditional

Medium Tempo

Will the cir cle be un bro ken bye and
bye Lord bye and bye There's a bet ter home a
wait ing in the sky Lord in the sky

G   G7
I was standing by my window
       C   G
On one cold and cloudy day
When I saw that hearse come rolling
                  D   G
For to carry my Mother away

Chorus

Will the circle be unbroken
By and by, Lord, by and by
There's a better home a waiting
In the sky, Lord, in the sky

Well, I told that undertaker
Undertaker please drive slow
For this body you are hauling
Lord, I hate to see it go
Chorus

I will follow close behind her
Try to hold on and be brave
But I could not hide my sorrow
When they laid her in her grave
Chorus

I went back home, Lord, home was lonesome
Miss my Mother she was gone
All my brothers, sisters crying
What a home so sad and alone
Chorus

Nitty Gritty Dirt Band / Will The Circle Be Unbroken
Ralph Stanley / Songs My Mother Taught Me And More
Joan Baez / Greatest Hits

147

Working On A Building

Traditional

Medium Tempo

If I was a singer I'll tell you what I would do
I'd quit my sinning and I'd work on the building, too

Chorus

I'm working on a building, I'm working on a building
I'm working on a building for my Lord, for my Lord
It's a holy ghost building, it's a holy ghost building
It's a holy ghost building for my Lord, for my Lord

If I was a gambler, I'll tell you what I would do
I'd quit my gambling and I'd work on the building, too
Chorus

If I was a drunkard, I'll tell you what I would do
I'd quit my drinking and I'd work on the building, too
Chorus

If I was a preacher, I'll tell you what I would do
I'd keep on preaching and I'd work on the building, too
Chorus

Ricky Skaggs / Rising Star
Seldom Scene / Old Train
Bill Monroe / The Music of Bill Monroe: 1970 - 1994
Stanley Brothers / Old Country Church
Chesapeake / Pier Pressure

148

Worried Man Blues

Traditional

Medium Tempo

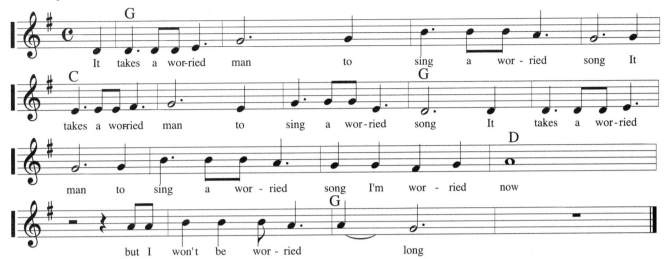

It takes a wor-ried man to sing a wor-ried song It takes a wor-ried man to sing a wor-ried song It takes a wor-ried man to sing a wor-ried song I'm wor-ried now but I won't be wor-ried long

^GIt takes a worried man to sing a worried song
^CIt takes a worried man to sing a worried s^Gong
It takes a worried man to sing a worried song
I'm worried n^Dow, but I won't be worried lo^Gng

I went across the river and I laid down to sleep
I went across the river and I laid down to sleep
I went across the river and I laid down to sleep
When I woke up, there were shackles on my feet

Twenty one links of chain around my leg
Twenty one links of chain around my leg
Twenty one links of chain around my leg
And on each link, the initials of my name

I asked the judge what's gonna be my fine
I asked the judge what's gonna be my fine
I asked the judge what's gonna be my fine
Twenty one years on the Rocky Mountain Line

If anyone should ask you who composed this song
If anyone should ask you who composed this song
If anyone should ask you who composed this song
Tell him it was I and I sing it all day long

149

Wreck Of The Old 97

Traditional

Oh, they $\overset{D}{\text{gave}}$ him his orders in $\overset{G}{\text{Monroe}}$, Virginia, saying,
"St$\overset{D}{\text{eve}}$, you're way behind ti$\overset{A}{\text{me}}$
This is n$\overset{D}{\text{ot}}$ 38, this is $\overset{G}{\text{Old}}$ 97
You must p$\overset{D}{\text{ut}}$ her into Sp$\overset{A}{\text{encer}}$ on ti$\overset{D}{\text{me}}$".

He turned and he said to his tired, greasy fireman,
"Shovel in a little more coal
And when we cross the White Oak Mountain
Just watch old 97 roll".

It's a mighty rough road from Lynchburg to Danville
A line on a three mile grade
It was on this grade that he lost his leverage
You can see what a jump he made

He was going down the grade making ninety miles an hour
When his whistle broke into a scream
He was found in the wreck with his hand on the throttle
Scalded to death by the steam

Now all you ladies, please take warning
From this time now and learn
Never speak harsh words to your true living husband
He may leave and never return

Flatt & Scruggs / Hard Travelin'
Norman & Nancy Blake / Blind Dog
Goose Island Ramblers / Best of the Goose Island Ramblers

Guitar Chords

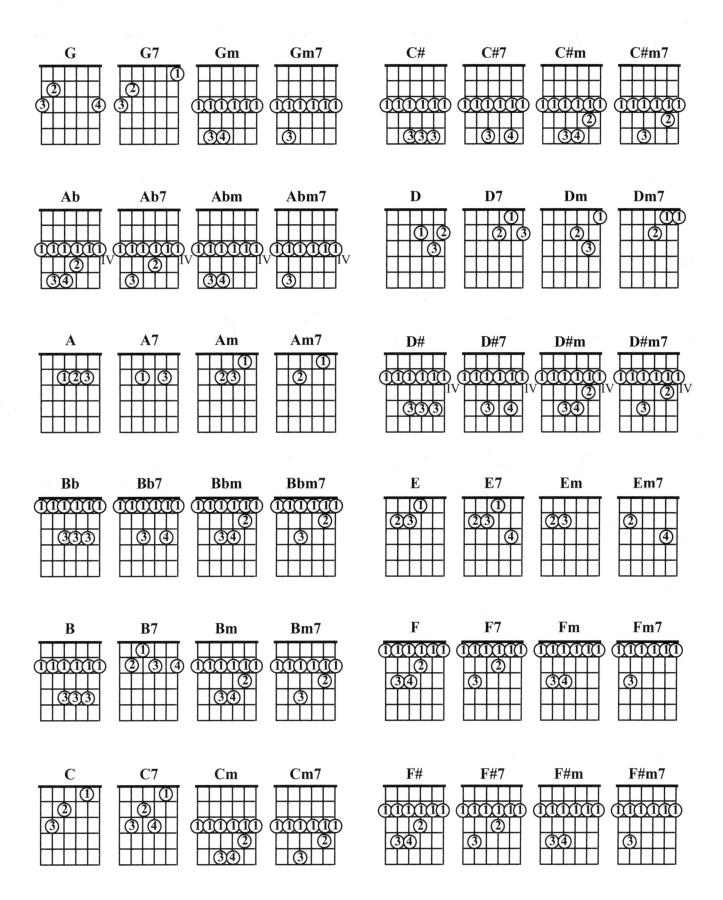

Mandolin Chords

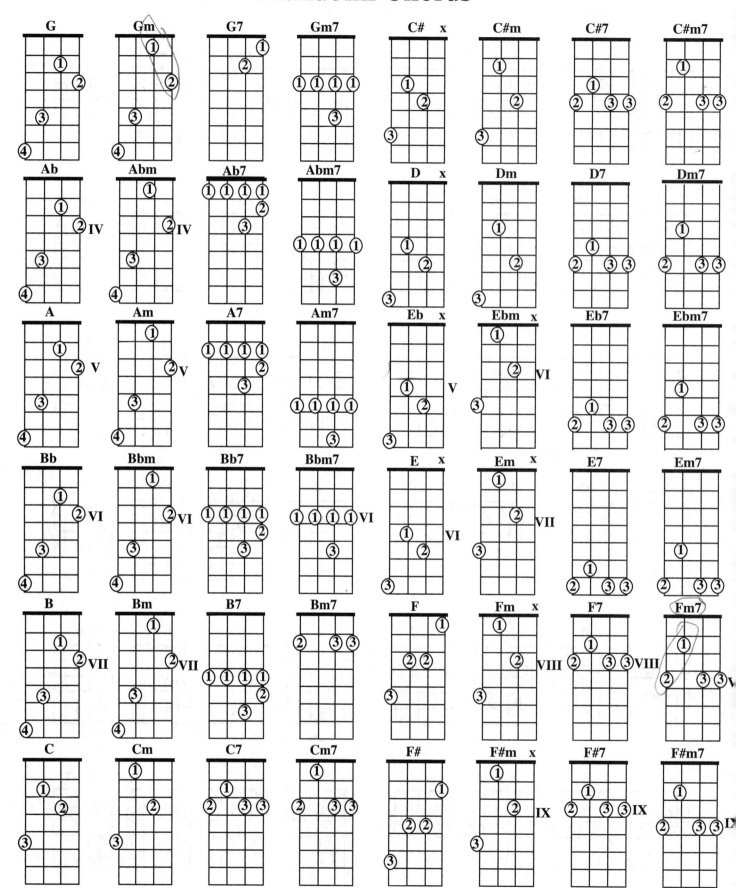

152

Banjo Chords

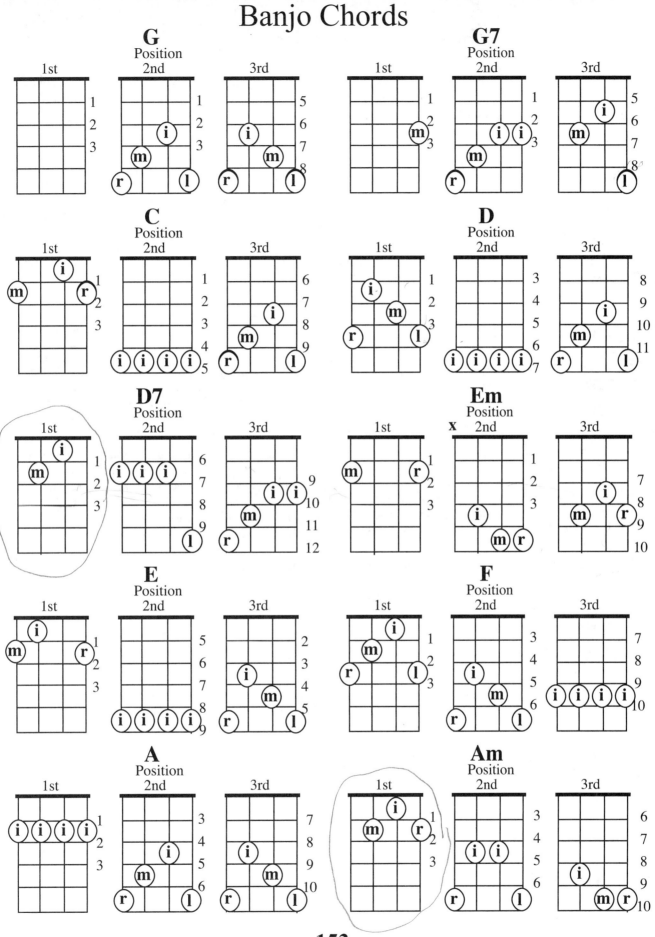

153

Other Bluegrass Products

Watch & Learn, Inc. offers the following products to enhance your bluegrass playing. The DVD & book/CD combinations are designed to be used together and include several of the songs in the *Bluegrass Fakebook*. Also, check out our websites for additional instruction - CVLS.com, FreeGuitarVideos.com, FreeBanjoVideos. com, and FreeMandolinVideos.com.

Books   DVDs

Acoustic Guitar Primer Deluxe Edition. Designed to take the beginner through the basics of playing bluegrass rhythm guitar. Covers proper hand positions, tuning, scales, rhythm (chords & strumming, bass notes, and bass runs) and lead playing. Utilizes many popular bluegrass standards to play and sing along with. Songs include *Tom Dooley, Going Down That Road, Worried Man Blues, Roll In My Sweet Baby's Arms, Banks of the Ohio, Dark Hollow, In The Pines, Amazing Grace, Pallet On Your Floor, Way Downtown, Sittin' On Top of the World, Wabash Cannonball, Crying Holy, Salt River, Billy In The Lowground, Little Maggie, Nine Pound Hammer, Wildwood Flower, John Hardy, Old Joe Clark, Blackberry Blossom, Will The Circle Be Unbroken.*
          Book/DVD/Jam CD $19.95

Flatpicking Guitar Songs book with CD is the follow up to *Acoustic Guitar Primer* and teaches how to become a flatpicker (lead bluegrass guitar). Includes exciting arrangements to popular songs written in both tablature and notation. There are several breaks for each song and each break is played slow (for practicing) and fast (for performing) on the audio CD. Songs include *Will The Circle Be Unbroken, Wildwood Flower, Home Sweet Home, Cripple Creek, Red Haired Boy, Nine Pound Hammer, Sally Goodin, Old Joe Clark, Black Mountain Rag, Salt River, Billy In The Lowground, John Hardy.* $14.95

Banjo Primer & Intro to Banjo DVD is designed to take the beginner through all the necessary steps to learn Scruggs style 5 string banjo, including proper hand position and techniques, 3 finger rolls, hammer ons, slides, pull offs, and bends. Learn to play 9 songs like the masters. Songs include *Boil Them Cabbage Down, Cripple Creek, Shady Grove, Worried Man Blues, Basic Breakdown, John Hardy, Black Mountain Rag, Kicking Mule, Little Maggie.*
          Book/CD $14.95   DVD $14.95   800-416-7088   *19.95
                                                                    6.50*

Mandolin Primer & Intro to Mandolin DVD teaches the beginner proper right and left hand technique while learning scales, how to solo, playing in four different keys, and playing rhythm using the mandolin "chop". Play along with 15 different songs. Songs include *Yankee Doodle, Oh Suzannah, Worried Man Blues, Wildwood Flower, Boil Them Cabbage Down, Cripple Creek, John Hardy, Red Haired Boy, Soldier's Joy, 8th of January, Blackberry Blossom, Bill Cheatum, Sally Goodin, Old Joe Clark, Salt Creek.*
          Book/CD $14.95   DVD $14.95

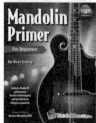

Fiddle Primer & Intro to Fiddle DVD is designed to teach the beginner how to read music, hold the instrument, develop proper bowing technique, and play in tune using many exercises and song examples. Contains 18 different fiddle tunes. Songs include *You Are My Sunshine, Wildwood Flower, Hot Corn Cold Corn, Amazing Grace, Blind Mary, Star of the County Down, Southwind, Will The Circle Be Unbroken, Angeline The Baker, Little Maggie, Boil Them Cabbage, Soldier's Joy, Cripple Creek, Red Haired Boy, Salt Creek, Roll In My Sweet Baby's Arms, Old Joe Clark.*
          Book/CD $14.95   DVD $14.95

Upright Bass Primer & Intro to Upright Bass DVD is designed to take the beginner through all of the necessary steps to learn the upright bass including how to hold the bass, locating notes, proper right and left hand technique, reading tablature, tuning, and playing simple walks. Play along songs include *Going Down That Road, Soldier's Joy, Tom Dooley, Nine Pound Hammer, Sittin' On Top of the World, Dark Hollow, John Hardy, Pretty Polly, Rueben's Train, Billy In The Lowground and Worried Man Blues.*
          Book/CD $14.95   DVD $14.95